EMPIRE OF CHAOS

SAMIR AMIN

EMPIRE OF

CHAOS

TRANSLATED BY W.H. LOCKE ANDERSON

MONTHLY REVIEW PRESS

NEW YORK

Copyright © 1992 by Samir Amin
Translation copyright © 1992 by Monthly Review Press

Library of Congress Cataloging-in-Publication Data

Amin, Samir.
    [Empire du chaos. English]
    Empire of chaos / Samir Amin ; translated by W.H. Locke Anderson.
       p. cm.
    Translation of: L'Empire du chaos.
    Includes bibliographical references.
    ISBN 0-85345-843-X : $22.00. — ISBN 0-85345-844-8 (pbk.) : $10.00
    1. Economic history—20th century. 2. Capitalism. 3. Socialism.
4. Democracy. 5. International economic integration. I. Title.
HC59.A785213 1992
337-dc20   92-9954
                                                            CIP

Monthly Review Press
122 West 27th Street
New York, NY 10001

10   9   8   7   6   5   4   3   2   1

CONTENTS

1. A World in Chaos   7

2. The New Capitalist Globalization   31

3. The Crisis of Socialism   56

4. The Democratic Challenge   82

5. The Regional Conflicts   102

1
A WORLD IN CHAOS

We all live on a planet whose destiny we collectively determine, or so we are told. And it is undeniable that the globalization which began five centuries ago with the European conquest of the Americas has passed into a new stage during the past forty years, as a consequence of the heightened intensity of international exchanges and the global spread of the means of destruction. Shall we conclude from this observation that all societies on the planet must subordinate themselves to the criteria of rationality that govern the global expansion of capital? This view, though dominant today, is not merely illogical and erroneous but infinitely dangerous.

Capitalism has always been a world system. The process of accumulation that governs its dynamic—shaped by a law of value that operates on a world scale limited to markets for commodities and capital to the exclusion of labor power—necessarily leads to the polarization of the world into center and periphery nations. Polarization is therefore immanent in capitalism and need not be explained by diverse and contingent factors peculiar to the social formations that make up the system. The recognition of this essential aspect of really existing capitalism has consequences that are as decisive for theoretical analysis as they are for the definition of progressive political action. For everything is subordinate to the logic of world polarization: the social struggles that develop in various local areas, the conflicts between states at the center, the forms of differentiation at the periphery, and much more.

This permanent trait of capitalism does not exclude change, which marks the successive phases of its expansion. For example, the long "Britannic empire" phase (1815-1914) was based on building a world market, particularly between 1848 and 1896. The market was structured by the contrast between the industrialized center—historically constituted as the base of the national bourgeois states—and the nonindustrialized periphery, which was gradually subjected to colonial and semi-colonial status. The world market under the hegemony of Britain went into crisis at the end of the period, owing to intensified rivalry from Germany and the United States. The system was gradually restructured by the retreats of the older imperial powers and their replacement by newer rivals in the crusade to carve up the world. This process led to World War I.

The breakup of the old system precipitated by the Russian Revolution and accentuated by the Chinese Revolution seemed to establish two systems, one of which styled itself socialist, although what really happened was basically the delinking of immense parts of the periphery. This long phase (1917-1980) can be divided into two periods. From 1914 to 1945, center stage was occupied by the violent conflict of the two world wars. Beginning in 1945, the world market then reconstructed itself under the hegemony of the United States, in an atmosphere of military and ideological bipolarization and cold war. During this entire phase the East-West conflict was presented as a struggle between socialism and capitalism, although it was never anything other than the conflict between the periphery and the center, manifested in its most radical form. This particular state of the world system provoked liberation struggles throughout the periphery, largely bourgeois in their orientation and capitalist in their aspirations. It was "the era of Bandung" (1955-1975), in which North-South conflicts were acted out within the framework of the East–West confrontation.[1]

The requirements of globalization during the postwar years, 1945-1970, were expressed in terms of a two-part paradigm. Within the developed countries it was thought that Keynesian interventions could assure steady growth to the benefit of all, dampening the business cycle and reducing unemployment to a minimum. This vision was all the more remarkable in that it envisioned simultaneously the reconciliation of national politics and the forward march of globalization. In the third world, the ideology of Bandung asserted that national development could be open to the advantages of economic interdependence. By contrast, the socialist countries were walled off in the ghetto of autarky.

The crisis of capitalism beginning in 1970 put an abrupt end to the illusions of Keynesianism and to what I call the ideology of development in the third world, while the so-called socialist countries had certainly not found the solution to their problems. But into the void created by this double crisis jumped the ideological offensive of neoliberalism, with its reductionist remedy for all ills, the market. Yet blind pursuit of this dogma could lead only to the breakup of the world system and the renewal of clashes between unbridled nationalisms, that is, to the opposite of what neoliberalism promised.

Globalization, which reestablished itself in 1945 and is now in a new phase, has assumed particular characteristics that sharply distinguish it from its earlier manifestations. The new globalization is characterized by a tri-polar constellation of the United States, Japan, and the European Community (EC) that is without precedent. This tri-polarity entails not only an intensification of trade among the poles but in particular an interpenetration of capital. Up until now, capital has always been national, but now it appears that a dominant international capital is emerging at an incredible rate. However, the alleged relationship between the change that operates on the level of property relations and the change that calls itself a "revolution in technology" has been inadequately analyzed, in my estimation, if indeed it actually exists. Each of the successive stages in the history of capitalism is defined simultaneously by its specific forms of domination of labor by capital and by the corresponding forms of existence of the bourgeoisie. One distinguishes, therefore, the phases of manufacture (1600-1800) and large-scale industry (1800-1920), both analyzed by Marx; and Taylorism-Fordism (1920-1980), analyzed by Harry Braverman.[2] The new stage, called "informationism," awaits analysis.[3] But while each of the three preceding phases operated within the framework of an "international economy" made up of certain key nations, I shall follow Michel Beaud and say that the new stage marks the emergence of a "world economy,"[4] i.e., a much deeper degree of integration.

The consequences of this change are major. Accumulation in the central nations was formerly regulated by national political and social conflicts that structured the hegemonic alliances. But there exists today no analogous mechanism that could structure such alliances on the grand scale of the economic decisions being made—not even for the United States–Japan–EC tri–polar cluster. Political analysts who see the dwindling scope of national decisions and the widening effects of an autonomous global economy are quite aware of this new fact. Yet there is no solution to the problem it raises, since no supranational state is visible on the horizon. This is the first major source of the chaos that the new globalization will bring in its train.

But it is not by any means the only source. The tri-polar penetration does not marginalize the periphery, as many economists suppose. Politicians, who are much more in touch with reality, refute this claim every day. The Gulf war illustrates the error. With four-fifths of the world's population—a vital reserve army of labor—and indispensible natural resources, the periphery must be preserved and subordinated to the expansion of capital, however polarizing this may be. This is the second source of chaos in the coming decades.

In a brilliant analysis of the history of globalization, Giovanni Arrighi has contrasted the contradictory effects of capitalist accumulation: at one pole the growing power of the active army of labor, at the other growing misery in the ranks of the reserve army.[5] The first tendency paved the way for social democratic strategies on the part of the masses, the second for revolutionary outbreaks of the Leninist type. I shall not go into this thesis at length, but I accept its essential claim. I only remark that Arrighi is too optimistic about the globalization that is under way, because he believes that it is going to draw together the active and reserve armies in the various regions of the system—the more advanced center as well as the periphery, and especially the semi-periphery. I do not believe it. On the contrary, it seems much more probable that geographic separation will continue to be dominant because the reserve army will remain concentrated at the periphery and semi-periphery. It follows that the ideological separation between social democracy at the center and the revolutionary attitudes at the periphery is not yet ready to disappear, even if the political forms of delinking produce something other than Leninist movements. As always, social democracy will remain limited in its capacity to move beyond the point it has reached and achieve the substitution of the hegemony of the salaried class for the hegemony of capital. (I shall return to this matter at a later point.)

Polarization, in my opinion, is a permanent and basic characteristic of really existing capitalism. It is not a cyclic phenomenon, as Arrighi suggests. He distinguishes, in effect, a sequence of periods: 1848-1896 (globalization); 1896-1948 (fragmentation of the world system); 1948 to the present (reconstruction of the world system). Be that as it may; I consider that the first of these periods is marked not by an accentuated contrast between the center and periphery, but by the emergence of the modern form of the periphery, which becomes colonial and semi-colonial. This development leads to fragmentation.

The Empire of Chaos

The world system is in crisis. There is a general breakdown of accumulation, in the sense that most of the social formations of the East (formerly called socialist) and the South (third and fourth worlds)[6] are unable to reproduce on an extended scale, or even in some cases to hold their own. The latter situation exists in the fourth world countries of Africa. In the fourth world the crisis manifests itself as an insufficiency of capital accumulation. In the developed center it takes an apparently opposite form that classical economics would call an excess supply of funds available for loans relative to the demand for productive investment. This excess is wasted in a wild orgy of financial speculation, creating an unprecedented situation.

The crisis reveals that the polarization of the world really constitutes a historic limit for capitalism. A genuine resumption of accumulation calls for a reallocation of capital on a global scale that is unattainable under the short-term profitability criteria that now rule the market. A market solution of the problem is bound to generate growing social, national, and international imbalances that will turn out to be unbearable. There is therefore no scientific value in neoliberalism, because it pretends not to see that the untrammeled market can only reproduce and deepen such negative consequences, and that an analysis of market advantages for a particular society is only valid to the extent that it starts from the real parameters of that society's situation: the level of its development, its historic place in the world division of labor, and the social and political links it has forged and maintained. A critical analysis must then ask what might make it possible to carry off a daring escape from the vicious circle of the market. From this point of view the considerable differences between various regions of the world imply specific political positions that cannot be derived from the postulated rationality of the market. To these objective factors one must add a quite valid recognition of the cultural, ideological, and political history of the various peoples. The real imperatives of our epoch imply therefore the reconstruction of the world system on a polycentric basis.

To any narrow political and strategic conception of the world order, such as that which centered on the Big Five (the United States, Europe, China, Japan, and the USSR),[7] it is vital to counterpose one that gives a real place to the nations and great regions of the third world. In that context the third world countries and regions have to subordinate their relations with others to the imperatives of internal development, and not the converse, which would compel them to adjust their international agendas to the world expansion of capital. This primacy of the internal imperative is the concept to which I apply the term "delinking," which clearly has nothing to do with exclusion or autarky.

Without a doubt this historic, fundamental limit to capital is tied in with other limits whose manifestations are quite plain to see, since they express themselves in certain "new" forms of social protest, rising sometimes to the point of questioning the legitimacy of the ideological and political systems of the advanced societies. The first such challenge is the refusal of workers and others to submit to the demands of economistic alienation. This refusal, clamorous during the revolts of 1968, lies dormant for long periods and then bursts out in dramatic and often destructive ways. The second is a response to the waste of natural resources and degradation of the natural environment by capital. It too has produced a movement, international in scope, that includes "green" political parties in some countries.

The crisis manifests itself along both geopolitical and cultural lines: in conflicts between states on the one hand, and in clashes of civilizations on the other. The response will therefore imply massive political changes, both the creation of new political organizations within the West, East, and South, and the reorganization of relations among them, i.e., a new interstate system. But none of these changes is on the agenda for actual political action. The historical drama of our epoch is situated here, and has its roots in the failure of social consciousness on the part of leaders who refuse to imagine positive and progressive alternatives.

The chaos results from a lack of correspondence between the geography of power on the one hand and the effects of the global expansion of capital on the other. The analysis of globalization I have proposed d ines the two spaces in which this lack of correspondence expresses itself: the relationships between the centers and their relationships to the peripheries. In my opinion, however, the intensity of the conflicts that arise in these two sectors is not equal.

The struggles for eventual leadership within the center— between the United States and its counterparts, Japan and Germany, between NATO and such military elements as survive in the USSR, and among the Europeans themselves— will remain limited. I can hardly imagine that they will lead to armed conflicts like those of 1914 and 1939. But neither will they find amicable solutions, for want of a coincidence between the arena of economic power and that of political and social decision-making. Neither the Group of Seven nor its veritable directorate (the United States, Japan, and Germany), even with all the infrastructure of institutionalized cooperation that exists in today's world, can render the social and political consequences of globalization unconditionally acceptable to all the participants. Nonetheless, because the conflicts of the developed West are not dramatic, they will resolve themselves by changes in the hierarchy of power without fundamentally questioning the internal social order the way it was questioned in Europe by the rise of fascism between the wars. There is a risk, however, that these conflicts will express themselves in part in the arena of North-South relations, in the characteristic conflict of actually existing capitalism, which opposes the people of the periphery and the expansion of world capitalism. In this context, who will win? Will the forces that would have a united North prevail over the South (as we saw to a startling degree in the Gulf war) win? Or will it be those advancing the cause of a polycentric world, in the sense in which I use the term? The future of humanity depends on the outcome: either an order more savage than ever, or an order that will ameliorate the intolerable contrasts between the center and the periphery. Only the latter outcome will open a humane perspective for future generations.

We are without doubt now marching down the wrong road. Liberal globalization will lead only to greater polarization, and by this act will summon up from the people of the periphery resistance movements which can only be massive and violent. But Western political thinking will ask only one question: How can one manage that which is intolerable? In this framework, the economic order produced by the world market (a grand disorder, in fact) must be capped with a military order that ensures the efficient repression of revolts in the South. The position of the Western powers on the reform of the international order therefore continues to be a refined hypocrisy, in which "morality," "law," and "justice" are invoked repeatedly in a futile attempt to mask the defense of unspeakable interests.

A NATO strategy corresponding to this vision of the world order already exists. It is based on a two-part program: one part that permits those festering situations in the third world that do not threaten the imperialist order, and a second that smashes by violent means—as we saw in the Gulf war—those emerging powers in the third world that rebel against this order.

Conflicts within the third world must be examined in this framework, for they are not all alike. There are conflicts that are the products of the objective impasses in which the societies of the third world are trapped by globalization, and conflicts stemming from the deficiencies of a social consciousness unable to respond constructively to such challenges. The drifts toward inter-ethnic or international conflicts are of this type. The mediocre political games of the dominant local classes feed on these drifts, and powers on the defensive turn their energies in these directions. Such conflicts do not menace the capitalist order. With a cynicism quite evident in their theory of "low-intensity conflict," the capitalist powers encourage such situations to develop. But some conflicts oppose the North directly to the South, either its popular force, or its state powers. Here, as we have already seen in the Gulf war, the rapid deployment tactical forces of NATO may be inadequate, and the strategy then taken by the Pentagon is violent in the extreme, to the point of genocide.

The efficacy of such strategies of intervention by the North requires the maintenance and reinforcement of Atlantic solidarity. But nothing beyond. The recognition of U.S. hegemony, perhaps restricted along military lines, leaves the field of economic competition open. The tacit accords with Japan, Germany, and other European powers, strengthened by the immobilization of the USSR and China, are enough. We see clearly now how the North-South conflict, an expression of the fundamental conflict of really existing capitalism, returns to center stage. For the détente and the rallying of the USSR to the tenets of the West provide no opportunity for the solution of regional conflicts, as the NATO propagandists proclaim. The North-South conflict has never been the product of the East-West conflict and its projection outside Europe, even though the support of the USSR for certain third world nationalist forces has sustained this impression. The North-South conflict is anterior and primordial; it has defined for five centuries capitalism as a polarizing world system, intolerable for this reason to the majority of the peoples of this planet.

This is why I shall express my conclusion on this theme in a manner brutal and simple in the extreme. The intervention of the North in the affairs of the South is—in all its aspects, at every moment, in whatever form, and *a fortiori* when it takes the form of a military or political intervention—negative. Never have the armies of the North brought peace, prosperity, or democracy to the peoples of Asia, Africa, or Latin America. In the future, as in the past five centuries, they can only bring to these peoples further servitude, the exploitation of their labor, the expropriation of their riches, and the denial of their rights. It is of the utmost importance that the progressive forces of the West understand this.

Problems Specific to Different Regions of the World

In the pervasive chaos of the present, one can distinguish problems of a general nature and problems that are specific to the regions comprising the contemporary world. The dominant discourse of the moment accents those of the first sort, ecology for example. Former President Mikhail Gorbachev himself, in the manifesto that established his popularity in the West, understood clearly the returns he could get by putting his deposits in this account. And these problems are real. But the fact remains that any response must be mediated by correct responses to the specific—and dramatic—problems of the diverse regions of the world, particularly the South and the East.

The countries of the East—the USSR and China—have launched reforms that assure the market and foreign trade a greater importance than they have had in the past. Their problem nevertheless has two faces that are inseparably linked: the democratization of society on the inside and the control of the overture to the outside. There is every reason to believe that the solution to this double problem is not reducible to the neoliberal recipe, but the right path to follow is difficult to spot. The uncertainty itself is twofold, existing both on the level of the social content of the system when it has regained its equilibrium, and on the level of its place in the world hierarchy. There is, to be sure, a direct link between these two levels, but it is difficult to establish until the question of "what it all means" has been answered. Will the critique of Stalinism work itself out in a return to capitalism, as the objective attitude once advanced by Gorbachev in the Soviet Union and Deng Xiaoping in China would lead us to believe? Or will it be derailed by a critique from the left, as Mao Zedong attempted in his day?

In the case of a return to capitalism, are peripheralization and the degraded international position that must accompany it inevitable? And how will the peoples of the USSR and China react? In the case of a progressive, national-popular advance, how will "conflicts in the bosom of the people" be managed and expressed in the face of objective economic laws, whether outside of or beyond actually existing capitalism? Such questions have yet to be answered.

I content myself here to enumerate such problems, and to return to them at a later time. However, I think it is useful to call attention to one point. In my previous analyses of the Soviet mode, I placed my emphasis on the three components of this system: capitalism, socialism, and statism. I now believe that the breakdown of this system leaves room for only two alternatives: (1) capitalism pure and simple, or (2) a national-popular evolution which establishes a balance between the forces and tendencies of capitalism and those of socialism. The dominant statism will have proven itself to be historically unstable, as Mao foresaw.

The developed societies of the West do have serious problems in common, although they lack the dramatic dimensions of those of the East and South. I propose to analyze them in terms of a crisis of Western democracy: how to assure within a democratic framework that the popular forces have access to political power?

This question has not yet been answered. The social democracy we have seen until now has permitted workers to achieve important social rights, although these are now the object of a capitalist offensive to dismantle them. However, in accepting the double consensus on which Western society rests—the regulation of political life by pluralist elections, of economic life by private property and the market—social democracy has not challenged the hegemony of capital, but only tempered it with the power of the workers in the political arena. On this level I do not share the optimism of Giovanni Arrighi, who seems to me to overestimate the strength and scope of workers' political power.

Western democracy, even now, is seriously troubled. With good reason the working classes judge with increasing severity what the pundits now call the "political class," whose right and left wings busy themselves with protecting the double consensus, draining all real content from "pluralist" politics. Systematic control and manipulation by the media, intended to prolong the life of the consensus, directs Western society on its gentle descent into a sort of saccharine fascism, paralyzing all hopes of a progressive evolution.

The historically necessary evolution should aim at substituting the hegemony of the salaried classes for the present historical compromise between labor and capital.[8] This will necessarily call into question the systems of ownership of the means of production and of economic decision-making. And at the ideological and cultural level it will challenge the technocratic vision of social control, as the Frankfurt School has called it for half a century. This is a long way off.

In the heart of the Western world, Europe faces challenges of its own. Building the Europe of the EC has been limited until now to the progressive widening of the market. But if, as in the phase of takeoff during the 1950s and 1960s, social adjustments to this widening could be made fairly easily, it is quite evident that entire regions and sectors would be unable to reconvert in the face of agonizing competitive challenges. As these challenges become socially and politically intolerable, they raise the possibility that the whole EC project may come tumbling down unless it is accepted that the market must be supplemented by plans for reconversion on the basis of a common progressive social policy. If such initiatives are undertaken by the European left, it will clearly demarcate its politics from neoliberal dogma and gain widespread support. But this is a long way off.

This first challenge had hardly been raised before the changes in the East confronted Europe with an equally grave challenge. The old European project, the EEC, supposed that the economic power of Germany (only West Germany at the time) would be counterbalanced by the political power of Great Britain and France. This possibility was foreclosed by German unification. The German choice—to invest its efforts in economic expansion toward the East and otherwise to stay in the shadow of the United States—emptied the European project of all its meaning.

The European project was from the outset an attempt to forestall the danger of "communism," now utterly gone, if indeed it ever existed. In this sense it was conceived as part of the economic, political, military, and ideological project of U.S. domination. An economically integrated Europe, never intended to be on a par with the United States, was to be just a subsector of the world system, open to militaristic Atlantism and to the economic penetration of U.S. corporations.

Europe continues to believe that it needs the military umbrella of the United States and therefore cannot afford to
break with Atlantism. Because of this view, any tendencies
toward autonomy, which had the apparent sympathies of
former French President Charles de Gaulle, never got beyond
the status of impulse. Eventually Europe was forced to rally
behind the United States and to again subjugate the third
world. NATO thereby became the instrument to breathe new
life into Atlantism.

With an exceptional lucidity, de Gaulle seized the two
essential givens of the problem. Right away he understood
Great Britain's historic choice, probably irreversible, to align
itself from 1945 with the United States, come what may. He
equally understood that it was necessary to conceive Europe
"from the Atlantic to the Urals," that is to say, on a scale that
would provide a counterbalance to the French-German *face
à face*. The changes in Eastern Europe should have given a
new vigor to this conceptual strategy. But European integration cannot be reduced to the expansion of the EC to the East.
The specific problems of the East are too grave for this limited
vision. Surely Gorbachev's proposal of a "common European home" responds to them. Even if his formula was
vague, it implied the development of institutions that allow
individual European states to respond to their particular
situations.

In my opinion, the only terms of a real alternative are:
either there will be a move toward the construction of this
common home, or Europe will come further apart—Germany going its own way, with or without the EC. It is my
impression that we are firmly embarked on this second path
for now.

The problems of the third world are major, and the new
globalization intensifies them further. Can the development

path taken by certain semi-peripheral states continue? In those that are already semi-industrialized, the development strategy is confronted with a decisive choice. Based on a distribution of income less and less egalitarian, such a path will clash more and more with emerging democratic aspirations. Whether or not these countries pursue progressive responses to their social problems, it is manifest that they will run head-on into the simple logic of globalization through the market. If they do nothing but succumb to adjustment, democracy will collapse before taking root. In other words, a stabilizing democracy along Western lines accompanying a capitalist path of economic development seems to me to be an illusion. Is it, moreover, a real objective of the Western powers? Or only a tactical diversion of the moment? The pursuit of industrial takeoff in the semi-peripheral states implies adjustment to a higher technology and containment of the class struggle within a democratic matrix. I do not believe that this will be easy or probable in any concrete situation I can think of.

The option of delinking, then, has no real alternative. To say it is not a genuine option is to say that there is no possibility but disintegration. Would it not be better to search for forms of delinking appropriate to the present circumstances than to succumb to chaos?

The prospects are even more somber for the African and Arabic South. When Great Britain and France were dividing these regions between them in the nineteenth century, they had no suspicion that one day they would have to accept their decolonization, as they did after World War II. The French could conceive of nothing better for their former empire in Black Africa than to place it at the disposal of the capitalists of the Community of Six, with France reserving particular privileges for itself by means of the franc zone,

Francophonism, and a system of defense agreements with client states. Neocolonialism thus took the place of the older type of colonialism.

The European plan for the Arab world and North Africa hardly went further, save that Europe had to keep the local ruling classes in a stronger position there than south of the Sahara. The implicit European strategy enmeshed the Arab nations in the impasse of a capitalism peripheral to European expansion. Although the petroleum nations could mobilize their financial means to accelerate industrialization, their ruling classes could only conceive of an industrialization which opened new outlets for the products of developed capitalism—European in particular, but also American and Japanese. This could only reinforce the tendency toward globalization, and was not in any sense progress toward autocentered national or regional development. When crisis came, this deepened integration in the global system showed itself to be catastrophic. Witness the foreign debt, whose effects were brutally aggravated by stagnation and the American counteroffensive. Saudi Arabia, a traditional client of Washington, opted for unconditional surrender to the financial and monetary instruments of American hegemony. Attempts at autocentered development had been partial, limited by the nature of the ruling classes of the nations that had begun them. Although a few gestures in this direction were made (and supported by the USSR), they were strenuously fought by the West, Europe included.

To what can we attribute this refusal of the Europeans to conceive of any relationship with the Arabs and Africans other than neo-imperialism?

An examination of the structural and conjunctural position of Europe will clarify this issue. Europe covers the deficit in its trade with the United States and Japan by means of a surplus in its trade with the third world and the East. In order to play the game of globalization, it needs to maintain unequal relations with its own dependencies. Europe, meanwhile, has found the principal opening for its expansion in modernizing its Southern European peripheries and its own industries. Unlike the United States and Japan, which predominantly exported capital in order to exploit the labor of the third world, Europe opened itself to massive importation of the manual labor it needed to fuel its own internal expansion. It is no accident that this immigration flows precisely from those European dependencies most damaged by this strategy: the Arab countries, Africa, and the Caribbean. It is also apparent that this immigration has created in Europe a political ambience hostile to the third world. Finally, since it is poor in natural resources relative to the United States, Europe attaches great importance to the security of its provisioning. Having renounced military autonomy, it has condemned itself to depend on the good will of the United States and to content itself with auxiliary rapid deployment forces (directed against the third world to complement those of the United States). This seems to constitute the extent of its military vision.

None of this gives credence to European pronouncements about the third world. In fact the Europe of the EC carries a heavy load of responsibility for the "fourth worldization" of Africa. For the unequal relations renewed by linking the EC and the ACP (the African, Caribbean, and Pacific countries associated with the EC) hardly constitute the liberation of Africa and the development of its people, but, on the contrary, imply their incarceration in mining and agriculture, as before. In this sense, Europe carries an important responsibility for the crystallization of the new dominant classes and the economic, social, and political disaster of the continent.

The ultimate alignment of Europe with the politics of adjustment advocated by the United States through the IMF and the World Bank illustrates Europe's conceptual mediocrity in this domain and shows clearly that the conflicts between the United States and Europe do not extend beyond narrow limits of commercial rivalry.

Europe's responsibility for the Arab impasse is also not negligible. Here too Europe has refused to depart from the strategy of the United States and its faithful instrument, Israel. The Gulf war tragically illustrates the consequences of this European choice. The objective is quite simply to maintain the Arab world in a state of maximal fragility and vulnerability by rejecting categorically even the idea of Arab unity (painted as a nightmare), by guaranteeing against winds and tides the survival of the archaic regimes of the Gulf, by assuring Israel absolute military superiority, and by denying the Palestinians the right to exist. Such unconditional support for Atlantism and Zionism has finally placed exclusive control over oil in the hands of Washington and reflects the limited capacity of Europe to rethink the Arab world. For a time, the Europe of the EC, at the initiative of France and its Mediterranean partners, toyed with the idea of "breaking" the Arab world by bringing the Mahgreb into its orbit. But the spontaneous reactions of the people of the Mahgreb to the Gulf war put an end to this unrealistic project.

There remains the failure of political and social consciousness that the Arabs share with other groups who respond inadequately to the Western challenge. Flights of archaic religious illusion, weaknesses in the forces of democracy, and the persistence of military autocracies have resulted from blocking alternative progressive perspectives in the Arab world. In this setting the building of a common European home should find its natural complement in a united

Arab world and a united Africa—the fundamental elements of a polycentric world. The way is long, and for now the chaos will persist.

The Way Out of the Impasse

In the preceding section I have tried to show that in all regions of the world the problems are serious, sometimes grave, and that for now the responses taking shape are not adequate to the challenges and do nothing but aggravate the chaos and barbarism. These deficiencies constitute the backdrop of the crisis of the left throughout the world.

The opposition of left and right reflects a double heritage in the capitalist world: the Enlightenment (conservatism versus progress and movement, authoritarianism versus democracy) and the workers' movement (the rationale of capital versus that of socialism). Neither element of this heritage is a decisive presence in the societies of the periphery. Here, the right-left boundary is drawn by acceptance or rejection of really existing capitalism, that is to say, the globalization that has peripheralized the third world. For this reason the national liberation movement, in all its historical forms—bourgeois, popular, and socialist—constitutes a force on the left side of the world ledger and the most active social force in the third world. The adversary it faces there is the class of ruling subalterns and compradors, whose qualifications are those of collaborators, traitors, or colonial lackeys, according to current usage. There is no consensus there such as structures the Western societies. Rather, in the conjuncture of current events, local power is in reactionary hands, whether well-established or shaky, or else it has reverted to the forces of a nationalist movement. The West invariably opposes such movements. In some manner one ought therefore to oppose the real monolithic quality of these Western societies—behind their glued-on facades of pluralism—to the genuine pluralism of opinion in the peripheral societies of the South and East, whose differences are too explosive to be managed by a Western democracy.

Contrary to a tenacious prejudice, the ideologies of national liberation movements do not attribute responsibility for their countries' situations to external factors. Quite the contrary, the emphasis is usually placed on combatting the local forces and ideas that constitute the obstacles to progress. But it goes without saying—at least that is the general opinion among widely diverse national liberation movements—that all progressive movements enter into conflict with forces that impose themselves from outside. The world capitalist system is therefore not considered to be a neutral or ambiguous factor and *a fortiori* is not positive. It is an obstacle whose name, imperialism—often dismissed with scorn in the West as "unscientific"—is in the peripheral states usual, banal, and general, an ever present influence regarded as self-evident. The internal quarrels that animate the movements of national liberation concern the concrete nature of this imperialism in each of the phases of the world expansion of capitalism since its origin: the forms of expression of the laws of its movement, the means of its intervention, the social alliances that it forges, and the means by which it reproduces polarization. There is, however, no doubt of imperialism's existence among its victims.

We know how difficult it has been and continues to be to establish a constructive dialogue between the left political groups in the West and those in the third world countries. Despite this fact, alas quite evident, the segments of the left most aware of the global nature of the challenge that humanity faces, and most committed to a universalist perspective, have always practiced this dialogue, whose vision extends well beyond the immediate results sometimes drawn from them.

A humane and progressive response to the problems of the contemporary world implies the construction of a popular internationalism that can engender a genuinely universalist value system, completing the unfinished projects of the Enlightenment and the socialist movement. This is the only way to build an effective front against the internationalism of capital and the false universalism of its value system.

On the internal level, social alliances which define the content of progressive strategies will necessarily produce alternatives for different regions. In the West, their bourgeois dimension—based on a long history that has led to advanced development—will remain prominent for quite a while. This does not preclude progressive socialization of the system and, in time, the emergence of the hegemony of the salaried strata. In the countries of the East, these alternatives will call for the liberation of society from the yoke of statism and a dialogue between socialism and capitalism. But in the third world, almost any alternative will imply reversal tendencies that are more radical than evolutionist, and the outright rejection of bourgeois subalternism. If, therefore, one is right to envision the substitution of popular control, national and regional, for the bourgeois vision of exclusive control by the market, the intense feeling of crisis which this choice implies will be more dramatic in the South and East than in the West. Failure to recognize this is sure to close off the response of people trapped in the hopelessness of antediluvian nationalisms and traditionalisms, whether religious or not.

The present crisis should be the occasion for the progress of critical thought, if one understands that to mean calling all dogmas into question. There is not much of this, perhaps because among other reasons neither academic economism nor the administrative mindset it engenders encourages questions. But the men and women who lead social movements and other progressive political forces are well aware of the need to question. The world polycentrism whose principles are outlined here is the only realistic basis for a new internationalism, and only the understanding that flows from its paradigm will equip us to recognize the objective diversity of our conditions and problems, to lay the foundations for reconstructing our world, and to acknowledge the common destiny of the peoples of our planet.

Notes

1. Samir Amin, "Bandung Trente Ans Aprés," in *L'échange inegal et la loi de valeur* (Paris: Economica, 1988).

2. Harry Braverman, *Labor and Monopoly Capital* (New York: Monthly Review Press, 1974).

3. I call attention to the pioneering work of Benjamin Coriat, *L'atelier et le robot* (Paris: Christian Bourgeois, 1989).

4. Michel Beaud, *L'économie mondial dans les années 80* (Paris: La Découverte, 1989).

5. Giovanni Arrighi, in Samir Amin, Giovanni Arrighi, Andre Gunder Frank, and Immanuel Wallerstein, *Transforming the Revolution* (New York: Monthly Review Press, 1990).

6. By "fourth world" I refer to those nations like Haiti and Sri Lanka which were formerly integrated into the capitalist system and have been marginalized by the resulting exhaustion of their natural resources.

7. Because the former Soviet Union remains in flux as I write this, I will use the designation "USSR" for clarity and convenience throughout this book.

8. Alain Lipietz has proposed this concept of the hegemony of the salaried classes in *Choisir l'audace* (Paris: La Découverte, 1989).

2
THE NEW CAPITALIST GLOBALIZATION

Abundant literature already exists about the economic evolution of the world over the course of recent decades; I shall only call attention to the essential givens of the present. To do this, I place in context, on the one hand, "trilateralization"(a barbarous term that designates the new interpenetration of the center economies, the United States, Japan, and the Europe of the EC), and on the other hand, the differentiations within the periphery. By this I mean the emergence of the semi-industrialized countries at one pole, and at the other, the destitute and discarded countries that comprise the fourth world.

Until the end of World War II, capitalism developed in its centers on the basis of bourgeois national states and was responsible for their emergence and evolution. The consolidation of the autocentered capitalist national economies was, in fact, the principal historical product of this development. In contrast, the world expansion of capitalism did not permit the periphery nations to constitute themselves in the same manner. But the "socialist" revolutions, like the movements of national liberation in the third world, proposed to construct such national, autocentered economies in one form or another; and this objective was the necessary precondition of genuine development.

The new globalization sets into motion the disintegration of these autocentered constructions at the very heart of the system in order to substitute for them a veritable world economy, to use the terminology of Michel Beaud. Is it necessary to accept this evolution as inevitable? Must one accept the dissolution of national structural integration when it exists as a historical heritage? Or forego its construction when it has not yet been realized? Is it necessary, in consequence, to substitute for former conceptions of development (always first and foremost national) a new vision set in the framework of global development? Or should one, and could one, reconcile some of the demands of globalization with the objective of national development, suitably redefined? Two responses to these questions exist and express different and conflicting social interests.

Whatever the facts, one response to this challenge which stands out entails substituting regional regroupings (more or less integrated) for the former autocentered nation-states. The European project constitutes the most evident of these aspirations, but it is possible there will be others. I should like to examine these responses to the challenge of globalization.

Globalization and Regional Performance

On initial examination, the large role foreign trade plays in the Gross Domestic Product (GDP) of various countries provides a measure of the level of transnationalization in the world's economic systems.

According to this criterion, transnationalization gained a stronger hold during the long cycle following the end of World War II. In addition, the slowdown in growth from the early 1970s on did not mean a slowdown in world trade, unlike the 1930s, when falling production was matched by declining external commerce. Rather, the reverse: the rate of expansion in external trade ran ahead of internal growth in the 1970s and 1980s.

In fact the proportion of exports in the GDP of the European countries comprising the Organization for Economic Cooperation and Development (OECD) rose from 12 percent in 1965 to 20 percent in 1988. If we take into account the increasing proportion of nonexportable services in the GDP (more than 60 percent), we have some measure of the decisive impact of external trade on agriculture and manufacturing. This is an altogether new phenomenon—although international competition as such is nothing new—and explains why the authorities have placed such stress on "international competitiveness" and have entirely abandoned the old maxim of national autonomy so prevalent in the 1930s.

It should be noted, however, that this intensified transnationalization is primarily a sign of the interpenetration of the developed capitalist economies, and only secondarily of North-South trade. World trade is expanding primarily because of the intensification of intra-European commerce encouraged by the EC. It is now possible to talk of a "European economic region"—although I would hesitate to describe it as an *integrated region* along the same lines as the great European national economies before World War II (Germany, Britain, and France). In addition, the expansion of world trade manifests the intensification of commerce among the three poles of the capitalist world—the United States, Japan, and the EC.

This shift is the main reason for the expansion of the proportion of world trade in the United States' GDP (from 6 percent in 1965 to 11 percent in 1988) and the rather more modest expansion in the world trade share of Japan's GDP (from 11 to 13 percent over the same period). If the EC is treated as a single country, disregarding intra-European trade, it can be seen that the external trade of each of the three giant poles represents about 12 percent of its GDP, while intra-polar flows account for more than 60 percent of total trade. This 12 percent figure comprises nearly a third of total industrial and agricultural production.

The flow of trade between the developed poles and the periphery is by no means insubstantial, despite the tendency to write it off that way. The third world is a significant and expanding market for the developed poles. It must be admitted that the expansion of this market is uneven in the extreme. In 1988, world trade (excluding the USSR, North Korea, the German Democratic Republic, Czechoslovakia, and Cuba) amounted to $2.6 trillion. The exports of the OECD comprised $2.0 trillion (77 percent) of this figure; the exports of China, $48 billion; India, $15 billion; other low-income countries, $45 billion; other middle-income countries, $341 billion; and the wealthy, underpopulated oil producers, $154 billion.

The intensification of international exchange and the interpenetration of national economies was fostered in the nonsocialist sphere after 1945 under U.S. hegemony. It was understood that the Europe of the Six, envisaged in 1958 by the Treaty of Rome, would extend this internationalization. Simultaneously, there appeared the beginning of an accelerated industrialization in certain countries and regions of the third world; and at almost the same time, the USSR, Eastern Europe, and China were pursuing an almost autarkic economic development that was probably more intense than that of the capitalist world.

These developments were abruptly modified beginning in 1970. At the outset, the capitalist world entered a crisis at the end of the 1960s. The long phase of sustained growth after World War II was over. After 1970 the average rate of GDP growth among the capitalist nations fell to two-thirds of what it had been in the preceding period; average growth rates of industrial and agricultural production fell to half. While conventional discourse persists in analyzing these changes from year to year in terms of the business cycle ("recession," "recovery,"etc.), what really lay behind the crisis was a long phase of structural transformation, and the deepening of globalization constituted a principal element. The restructuring had further dimensions, of course, technological and otherwise. However, the attention focused on the collapse of the systems called socialist and the financial aspect of the world crisis (indebtedness, exchange rate fluctuations, inflation, etc.) often made one forget the real basis of the structural crisis around which the conjunctural changes revolved.

The collapse of the economic (and political) systems of Eastern Europe and the uncertain futures of the USSR and China constitute the second dimension of the structural transformation that is under way. In the USSR and Eastern Europe the rhythms of growth died down in the second half of the 1980s and led to the present crisis. In China, by contrast, these rhythms have remained strong since the 1950s, through the ups and downs of political struggle; perhaps they even accelerated in the 1980s. The crisis of the system is, accordingly, of a different nature from that which batters the USSR and Eastern Europe, despite the confusion produced in this domain by the dominant political prejudices.

The third element of the new situation is the contrasting

evolutions of the different regions of the capitalist third world. I call particular attention to the elements of evolution in the periphery pertaining to the fundamental questions posed above: What is the nature of this development? What are its contradictions and its limits? Can one envision the pursuit of development subject to the constraints of globalization? Can one substitute a different perspective?

I shall first examine the economic performance of the third world in the strictly conventional terms of growth and external balance, particularly for the 1980s decade. From this standpoint these performances are as a whole mediocre, and in some cases calamitous. The rates of growth are low everywhere except India and East Asia. And this collapse of growth is disastrous for the countries of the fourth world. Sub-Saharan Africa recorded enormous declines in real per capita income on average over several years. The same is true for the third world countries as a whole, even for the so-called middle income countries. The 1980s were marked by a fall in per capita income in Latin America, which was catastrophic for the heavily indebted countries, as the adjustments imposed on them called for reductions in productive capacity. Even countries with industrial exports saw a slowdown in growth, although it remained positive on a per capita basis.

Other conventional indicators also confirm this picture. The rate of accumulation suffered from the fall in income. The statistics here are unreliable, but indicate probable stagnation at a low level, more severe in the poorer countries and the debtor countries most heavily affected by the necessity for "adjustments." Conversely, an increased investment rate was recorded in India and was particularly marked in East Asia. It must be understood that the investments required by modern industry, especially the export industries, are increasingly costly. Under these circumstances, stagnation in spending often means negative net investment. A marginally improved rate of investment may produce only mediocre production gains relative to the exports necessary to pay for it. The World Bank has nothing to say on these points, since they run counter to its dogma.

The results measured in terms of export growth must, of course, be judged against their investment cost. Exports are up almost everywhere in proportion to GDP, even if they are stagnant for the poorest countries. They are up even more in India, in the middle income countries in general, and particularly for the industrial exporters of East Asia. But at what cost for society? The cost of foreign indebtedness, of which investment is one of the causes. The literature on debt is so plentiful that it is not worth adding anything here.

There are additional damaging effects of the general crisis and the third world's burden. Statistics on the share of administrative costs in the typical third world nation's GDP reveal only a fragment of the state's role and the social services it provides. If there is a casual tendency to say that the state is top-heavy in the third world, the relative burden of the state on the national economy is still much lower throughout this region than in the countries of the OECD. Undoubtedly, the state burden is more difficult to carry in the poor countries owing to the relatively small proportion of their output that consists of commodities. But the real issue is the quality of state services, their efficiency, and their social effect. State intervention that is considered inefficient by the foreign "experts" is perfectly understandable and effective by the criteria of the social and political functions it fulfills.

By the conventional criteria of liberal economics, the economic performances of the countries of the third world are mediocre or disastrous. But increasing transnationalization is not a healthy response to the crisis; it is an ingredient. According to the conventional view, there are really only two exceptions to the general failure of development, India and East Asia.

Adjustment Versus Development

It is fashionable nowadays to draw two dogmatic conclusions from the facts. The first is that transnationalization is ineluctable and must be accepted as such, the only solution being *adjustment*. The second is that active adjustment to the demands of transnationalization is possible on the part of the so-called developing countries, and that the "success" of South Korea and a few others provides the evidence for this. The World Bank reports are models of this kind of thinking. Reading them—a task about as rewarding as reading *Pravda* in the 1960s—is a good game for the practiced, who can usually guess in advance what the Bank will say on any topic. The real issues are always fudged and the false issues addressed in terms of the litanies of adjustment, supported by mountains of data. These data are the only useful parts of the reports, although they are often silent on the key aspects of the genuine issues. Econometric models, never more than pretentious substitutes for back-of-the-envelope calculations, are always manipulated to say what their authors know, irrespective of the data.

We must look beyond the conventional criteria and take a perspective longer than that of what I call really existing capitalism. For this purpose attention must be paid to what conventional analysis ignores: income distribution, employment, training, social services, the position of the state, development contradictions (especially between the town and the countryside), and so on. An income distribution acceptable to the nation as a whole is an absolute essential; without it there is no nation. The nation cannot exist without substantial control over its technology, finance, food supply, industry, military hardware, and culture. Without this autonomy, the nation is not an active agent in shaping either world society or the vital aspects of its own history. The frustrations of forced surrender to an evolution it cannot control have severely damaging effects. A country's performance in the world economy must be assessed against a background of these considerations. Has the growth in question taken place under conditions that have exacerbated contradictions, sharpened disparities, and deepened dependence; or has it been genuinely autonomous development?

Data supplied by conventional economics provide no answers to these questions. The statistical appendices of the World Bank reports provide only limited usefulness. They can be quickly scanned. As for the gloss the World Bank chooses to impose, it is vacuous, irrelevant, and inappropriate in its use of data, its main function being to legitimate the Bank's own dogmas. From time to time the Bank inveighs on issues such as poverty, but the very term belongs less to social science than to the decorous chitchat of the social gala. Needless to say, there is no recognition that the poverty in question is the product of policies prescribed by the Bank itself.

Disparities in the distribution of income are acute everywhere in the third world, even in India, and tend to be worst in those countries with the most pronounced growth. The only exceptions are South Korea and Taiwan. Admittedly, the degree of disparity is variable, with Latin America enjoying the dubious distinction of having the most deplorable conditions of all. Liberals, meanwhile, soothe their consciences with the thought that it was the same in Europe at the birth of capitalism. But they fail to note that gradual improvements in the conditions of Europe's working classes were won chiefly through their own struggles (the kind that liberals condemn in the third world), waged in the context of an imperialist expansion that facilitated their success. The inexorable law of accumulation, as formulated by Marx, operates more on the world scale of really existing capitalism than it does on that of its centers taken in isolation.[1] What liberals seem to forget is that the increasing disparity observed at the periphery of the system is not a vestige of a precapitalist past (the fashionable neo-Weberian thesis), but the inevitable product of the capitalist present. They also forget that accumulation on a world scale produces structures at the periphery that are not conducive to struggles like those that occurred in the West.

Other indicators register the negative impact of the law of increasing disparity associated with capitalist expansion at the periphery. In the first instance there is unemployment, whose real extent is in no way reflected by official statistics. In actuality unemployment exists on an enormous scale in the capital cities of the third world (30 to 50 percent of the potentially active population is a reasonable estimate). And feverish urbanization runs well ahead of the level of development. Overall, the urban population accounts for at least half the total population in Latin America and the Arab world, and approaches half of the total in an increasing number of other areas. What is clear is that this drift to the towns indicates social contradictions beyond the control of capitalist expansion, aggravated, particularly in Africa, by the destruction of rural societies in the wake of urbanization.

Under such circumstances, progress for the third world requires opposing the law of accumulation, not "adjusting" to it. This conclusion is valid whether development takes place within an overtly capitalist framework or evolves under the authority of popular social fronts. It also explains the success of South Korea and Taiwan, which went against the prevailing winds and the liberal social prescriptions.

Accordingly, "dependency," which is supposedly out of fashion, is a glaring fact, and its intensification is confirmed by all the studies of the "technology gap," foreign debt, models of globalization diffused by the mass media, and so on. This dependency is neither the cause nor the effect of disparities in income distribution. Along with the disparity to which it is closely linked, dependency is inherent in the world expansion of capitalism. It is one side of a coin whose other side is the compradorization of the privileged classes, who benefit from the expansion and are the transmitters of dependency, not its victims.

Solving these problems requires control over foreign relations and the state's active intervention in production guidelines, social distribution, research and development, employment and training, and the like. When the World Bank and Western agencies argue that the "poverty trap" can be resolved without challenging liberal dogma, by juggling the various recipes that have been in and out of fashion, they are promoting failure. The Bank frequently follows this line of thinking, without self-criticism for the failures it has personally encouraged.

China so far seems to be the only *clear* exception to the comprador option. It might therefore be able in future to play the subtle game of a more pronounced integration into the world economy without having to forego its own national self-reliance. Everything will depend on internal political changes. In this instance, since there has been delinking, in my sense of the word, the internal factor has once more become crucial.

Other alternatives to compradorization must be distinguished in subtly different ways. Cuba and Vietnam are resistant, but isolated to a degree that is partly of their own choosing and partly imposed by an imperialism that has not given up hope of breaking the national will of "small countries."India's performance, even if it falls far below China's, is better than that of the capitalist third world as a whole. India has not suffered from the crisis, and has maintained its rate of growth. This is certainly an effect of its great size and the autonomy and self-reliance such size allows—precisely the opposite of what liberal dogma suggests. However, India remains fragile, and its future will be uncertain as the Jawaharlal Nehru/Indira Gandhi style of nationalist ideology is worn away by the aspirations of the comprador bourgeoisie and the challenge of local nationalism. South Korea and Taiwan are even more exceptional, as they are in principle anti-socialist. What is surprising in both cases is not the achievement of rapid growth without damage to the nation's balance of payments—something that other countries have managed—but the centering of the nation around a strong state while maintaining reasonable equity in income distribution—something other countries have not done. Again, their success stems from doing the very opposite of what the prevailing liberal dogma urges them to do.

There is really no other exception in the capitalist third world: the wealthy countries (the oil producers, for example); the poor countries; countries congratulated by the World Bank on their "success" in terms of growth and external balance of trade, the only criteria liberalism recognizes; and those unfortunate countries that have expired under liberal treatment and now comprise much of the fourth world. There is no encouragement here for talk of success in terms of a strengthened national construct. Even in the semi-industrialized countries pinpointed by the World Bank (Brazil, Mexico, Turkey, Thailand, etc.), and in countries such as the Ivory Coast and Kenya, there has been little progress in nation-building. On the contrary, the widening disparity in income distribution is in this regard a sign of failure. It reduces the chances of social integration, without which nation-building is meaningless.

Each case must be treated individually, of course. Here and there some elements of a national policy can be discerned. In newly industrializing countries (NICs) there is technological or financial control. In others with nationalist traditions the state plays a part in industrialization or land reform. But these elements have not generally achieved the critical mass essential to counteract the comprador ambitions of the privileged classes. Accordingly, any progress is fragile and threatened with the dismantling that the World Bank advises.

The best Indian analyses (for example, that of Amiya Bagchi) criticize the results and the vulnerability of the Indian model much more severely than those of the majority of foreigners, who are often victims of the "myth of Nehru."[2] Nehru's statism was open to big capital, both Indian and imperialist, and the social reforms remained modest, never threatening the great landowners of the North and always remaining weak in their capacity to absorb technology. Moreover, the drift to the right, marked in the later years, inscribed itself in the logic of the internal evolution of the system. Liberalization under these circumstances led more in the direction of "predatory commercialization" (the term employed by Bagchi) than of entrepreneurial initiatives. The pauperization that followed was more than an acceleration of proletarianization. It produced regional irredentisms and cliques, thereby weakening the pan-Indian alliances that centered on big local capital, landed property, and the techno-bureaucracy.

The judgments passed on the newly industrializing countries of Southeast Asia (Thailand, Malaysia, Indonesia, and the Philippines) by critics are no less severe.[3] This model is defined by three components: a technocratic-economistic vision of development inspired by the World Bank, a consumerism of the urban classes, and a police-state doctrine of national security hostile to all democratization. This model was sustained by Western aid during the 1960s, followed by foreign borrowing in the 1970s, while its widespread industry based on low-cost handicraft methods was forced into crisis by the progress of automation in the developed centers. One critic, Yoshikara Kunio, does not hesitate to call this construction, so vaunted by Western experts, "ersatz capitalism," vulnerable because it lacked the technological capacity to respond to the challenge of modernization.[4]

China and India

In view of the exceptionally large populations concerned, evolution and progress in China and India are essential to the future of the world system. In this context, any comparison is overwhelmingly in China's favor.

The traditional criteria of economics are a primary element in the comparison. For the long period 1950-1990, China showed a rate of growth in GDP two to three times that of India. Its exports (especially of industrial goods) were double those of India in relative terms, its investment rate one-and-a-half times. China's burden of debt service was also only a third that of India's.

There is no need to examine statistics to see that the income distributions of the two countries differ drastically. Nowhere in China does one observe the appalling wretchedness of living conditions found everywhere in India. It is more difficult to make a judgment as to the degree of dependence on external forces. The great leap in China's exports in the 1980s, it can be noted, was the result of an autonomously determined policy. The almost total embargo on foreign trade imposed by the imperialist powers in the 1950s and 1960s was used extensively by the Chinese to encourage self-reliance and embark on gigantic, progressive social changes remote from the constraints of external pressures. However, Soviet aid in the 1950s was by no means a negligible factor in the first installment of industrial, technological, and military capability. Later, a leap in imports matched by exports was a necessary part of the "four modernizations"under Zhou Enlai. Was the opening to the world controlled? That is hard to say, as its damaging effects were often felt through the subtle channels of the consumption patterns of the privileged. Nevertheless, the nature of power in China, which is not exercised directly and exclusively by the bourgeoisie as in India, has so far limited the destructive impact of the international environment.

Europe and the Challenge of Civilization

The fundamental issue—the contradiction between transnationalization and national autonomy—gives rise to divergent positions from the outset. The potential in this historical project is vastly different from that imagined by proponents of a traditional response. Yet all authorities in the OECD countries—and behind them a public opinion largely shaped by those authorities—apparently go along with the principle of evolution from an international economy to a world economy. The right and the left, as they are defined in Western electoral politics, totally agree.

Behind this unanimous facade stand shades of meaning quintessential to the political changes in the foreseeable future. The United States and Japan are not merely geographical areas of a world economy that is under construction. They are and will remain national economies, with a state that ensures the continuance of national structures while grabbing the lion's share of world trade. Fanatics of liberalism will tell us that this is a rearguard action. It may come down to this over the next couple of centuries, but it is a vanguard action from the perspective of the next couple of decades. These national options remain decisive at such levels as: spending on research, development, and labor force retraining; *de facto* protection of agriculture; mineral and oil resource development; and even manufacturing and financial management. On top of this, the United States holds a trump card as long as the dollar fulfills the role of world currency.

Europe's situation is by no means comparable, and it cannot be argued that building the EC will make it such. Europe is a creature of its past, of the coming together of historically constituted national economies. The EC is not a supranational state, and the common policies—even under the single market of 1992—do not make it such. There is no common policy except the subsidization of agriculture, which is threatened, as it is in the United States. The elements of an overall monetary policy are weakened by a diversity of anti-inflationary and short-term policies, not to mention the absence of even a plan for a common social policy. For the foreseeable future the common market is what the name suggests and nothing more. Integration by means of a market creates more contradictions than it resolves. It runs the risk of weakening Europe as a whole by strengthening some countries while debilitating others. This process proceeds to the point where the national structures of the strong are maintained and those of the weak are eroded, without leading to an integrated whole.

This less-than-optimistic prospect is made more likely by the persistence of contradictory national strategies within the EC. Britain accepts worldwide expansion and erosion of national power, but not to the benefit of a European construct. On the one hand it is open to a world without borders, as it adopts information technology from Japan over technology from Europe. On the other hand, Britain is profiting from its legacy as a powerful financial center that has always bowed to the prospect of being swallowed by the United States, owing to its shared language and culture. On this count, the European construct will remain handicapped by linguistic diversity. It is hard to imagine a common research and development effort and common systems of worker training. In what language would they be conducted?

At the other extreme, Germany is in an entirely new situation. West Germany was already the economic giant of the EC, with manufacturing exports on a par with those of the United States and Japan, and more than double those of Britain, France, and Italy. But it was regarded as something of a political pygmy. The EC's power balance depended on these compensating factors: Britain and France in the political driver's seat and the German economy as the engine. Under the new circumstances, a unified Germany could almost go it alone. This means that Germany, without raising a formal objection to the EC, might want to push European integration no further than a common market. As the strong partner, it may accept market rules and retain the integrity of its national structures while those of its partners erode. It may even reinforce its position of strength by expanding its influence in Eastern Europe.

Between the British and German options, there is no space for a third. France, Italy, and other members may dream of activating a European political structure to offset their economic weaknesses through political commitment. But can such dreams be anything more than pious hope?

The future of the German plan depends finally on what Germany decides. If it decides to go it alone, it could become a third pole of an economic *and* political system that also includes the United States and Japan. Of course it would have to overcome some obstacles. German technology does not equal that of the other two nations, and its export performance is based on the traditional industries of post-World War II reconstruction rather than the new technology. But Germany has not yet resumed its proper political role. Britain and France are permanent members of the UN Security Council, with the right of veto, although this privilege is probably on its way out.

So why should Germany not exercise the "European option," as its chancellor has proclaimed? More to the point, why should it? It would only maintain the political privileges of its partners with nothing in return for itself that was not there for the taking anyhow.

Pending these decisions, it has to be admitted that even collectively Europe remains a political pygmy, as Germany by itself has hitherto been described. Europe under the U.S. nuclear umbrella (worthless at this point with the end of the cycle of deterrence),[5] and fragmented by the divergent foreign policies of its member states, has been able to make little more than a rhetorical stand against the United States. Its weakness bars it from a major role in settling North-South issues, such as the Palestine question. On most questions it has to fall in line with decisions made in Washington, as the Gulf crisis demonstrated.

For Europe to become a third pole, with the consequent opportunity of being the principal pole on a world scale, it must pursue de Gaulle's dream of a Europe "from the Atlantic to the Urals" (or Vladivostok). Gorbachev is the only person who has expressed this vision recently, in his concept of a "common European home." This recipe for reconciling transnationalization and national autonomy is a confederal vision, allowing the British, French, Germans, Russians, and others room to respond to their varying objective circumstances. It is also, I believe, close to the desires of those of a cosmopolitan turn of mind who are not willing to cut loose from their national, historical roots.

Towards a Regionalization of the Global System?

If we look simultaneously at intra-EC trade, trade among the poles (the United States, Japan, and the EC), and trade among the semi-industrialized regions of the third world, we can see how regional crystallization fits into the framework of increasing transnationalization. Crystallization occurs around each of the poles, but the respective peripheral states enjoy very different possibilities.

The North American region, comprised of the United States and its "external province" of Canada, is the natural partner of Latin America and the Caribbean. Mexico is already on the road to complete integration into the North American market. Central and South America are being encouraged to follow this example, and there is a proposal for a free trade area stretching from Alaska to Tierra del Fuego.

The great East and Southeast Asian region dominated by

Japan is in the process of incorporating its semi-industrial-ized countries (Thailand, Malaysia, Indonesia, and the Phil-ippines), but the exact boundaries of the region are still undetermined. It is by no means clear that South Korea can be regarded as integrated into this region any more than China is. Even India, with all its weaknesses, retains its autonomy from the Japanese pole. But the "Japanese" region could stretch westward to include Burma, Sri Lanka, and even Pakistan and the Gulf.

The region around the EC has its own shape. It is formal-ized in the EC's association with the African, Caribbean, and Pacific countries that comprise the ACP. But the African periphery nations affected are essentially the poorest coun-tries, whose potential within the existing system is unprom-ising. This is, no doubt, why trade between the EC and the South is relatively less substantial than that between the United States and Japan and the South. Europe has concen-trated on its own integration, which received a boost in 1992 with the launching of the single market. Europe's opening of its eastern frontier also may provide new prospects for inte-grated European expansion and a further slowdown in the growth of trade between Europe and the South.

It is therefore premature to talk of "regionalization" within transnationalization. The peripheral nations are still largely exposed to the competition among poles vying for a place in their goods and financial markets. The competitiveness of the poles is different in different markets. Japan and the United States have the edge in new technologies, especially in infor-mation processing. The United States, Canada, and France have the advantage in grain production. Germany is pre-dominant in traditional mechanical engineering and chem-istry. France is in the forefront in some armaments, railways, and aeronautics. Trade between the poles differs from their separate trade with the periphery. Comparative advantage in new technologies is crucial in inter-polar trade, much less so in competition for third world markets.

But the chief obstacle to discussion of regionalization as an accomplished fact is the enormous uncertainty hanging over the policies of the Soviet Union, China, India, and the third world, to say nothing of uncertainty about the future of Europe itself and the crucial decisions to be made by the new Germany. In these matters we can only conjecture. A unified Germany's bid for expansion to the east will have a profound effect on Germany's own integration in the EC. It seems to me that the Soviet Union, China, and even India will cling to the possibility of remaining independent from any specific pole, and that by that token they will retain significant room for maneuver. In comparison, it does not seem to me probable that the great regions of the third world—Latin America, the Arab world, Africa, or Southeast Asia—will organize themselves as independent regions. However, it is only such polycentric regionalization that can provide an alternative to worldwide capitalist expansion.

I should add that despite verbal declarations to the contrary, Western power politics are persistently and fundamentally hostile to all regional realignments in the third world, as they are toward anything that might strengthen the autonomy of the third world in general.

I shall give an example of this hostility—the European hostility toward the unity of the Arab South. (With some obvious qualifications, the question of African unity is quite similar to that of Arab unity.) Yet the building of Arab unity is just the turning point needed for progress toward the polycentric ideal. Is it not a commonplace that the balkanization of the region stands in the way of modern development? In a progressive vision of a common future, in the serious sense of the term, Europeans and Arabs must accept their mutual dependence by affirming their respective regional unities and ceasing to see them as dangers.

To be sure, Arab unity is not the order of the day, and in politics one must be realistic. The powers that be in the Arab countries, compradorized as they are, cannot conceive of it. But how fragile are these powers, as we saw during the Gulf war! It is well understood that the road to building Arab unity—an absolute requirement for solving the problems of the Arab people, which have the highest priority of the problems of our epoch—is a long one. It is not possible to think of Arab unity as coming about the way that unity in Germany did in the nineteenth century, through Prussian conquest. The error of dictators such as Saddam Hussein is not to understand this. The only path is that of democracy, of progressive social transformations, of respect for local interests, although this way is not a utopia. The Arabs will have less difficulty achieving unity than did the Europeans, who did not have the advantage of common language and culture that the Arabs have.

It seems dangerous to me that the dominant political and ideological forces on the European left (and right) cannot imagine that Arab unity could be desirable. Europe has not yet thrown off its imperialist tradition that the "other" is an enemy that must be kept weak and divided, especially if this other is culturally different. The world order of really existing capitalism rests on this fundamental principle and nothing indicates that it is about to change.

For half a century this world order has pursued a single overriding objective in the Middle East, to perpetuate what is euphemistically called "access to oil," under terms that unmistakably ensure the command of the Western powers over this resource. To attain this objective, two complementary means have been employed: first, the perpetuation of the division of the Arab world and the assured survival of the archaic regimes of the Gulf—Saudi Arabia, Kuwait, the Emirates, and Qatar—in a manner that precludes any possibility that their petro-wealth will be used in the service of all the Arab peoples; and second, the guarantee of the absolute military supremacy of Israel (which has been helped to arm itself with nuclear weapons) in a manner that gives it the power to intervene instantaneously whenever it wants to. The Gulf war showed that Europe has no concept of its own of relations with the Arab world different from that of the United States.

The different scenarios considered for the future of North-South relations can now be reread in the light of these reflections. The criteria for distinguishing among these scenarios are always in the last analysis the degree of autonomy of Western Europe from the United States and the degree of regionalization at the heart of the world system which can go along with it.

The scenario of a collective European neo-imperialism dominating "its" Arab and African South may still flatter those who pine for what has long since passed away, but the Gulf war demonstrated that such a scenario has no substance. If the oil is to be controlled by the West, it will have to be done directly by the U.S. military. And Europe has no card to play against such a project other than amity with the Arab peoples. This choice is not open. Since 1945 Great Britain has been selling itself to the United States on the installment plan; Germany, which is preoccupied with its economic expansion to the East, will continue to maintain a low profile; France, having renounced de Gaulle's principle of refusing to adapt French interests to those of the United States and Israel, is by this fact marginalized.

In all these domains the politics of Europe is remarkably mediocre. With France at the forefront, followed by Italy and Spain, Europe has toyed with the idea of "breaking" the potential unity of the Arabs by offering the ruling classes of North Africa a seat on the European train, while leaving the Arabs of the East under the domination of Israel. The Gulf war has put an end to this project by solidifying the Arab world. In Sub-Saharan Africa, European politics are content to maintain the existing regimes in place if they are dictatorial, thereby making more difficult the indispensable unity of the region.

The regionalization at the heart of the world system remains quite relative. Although it is true that the United States weighs heavily on Latin America and Japan on Southeast Asia, the Arab world does not appear in the sphere of influence of the EC, but in that of the United States. The sphere of influence that is properly "European" may soon be reduced to the African fourth world. Germany, moreover, appears to be aware of this fact and to be acting accordingly. As for the USSR, it is still far from being able to regain a presence outside its own borders. For the near term, Europe will not exist "politically."

In fact, the hostility of Europe to Arab unity is the product of its Atlantism and its support for the expansionist aspirations of Israel. The United States and Israel see their interests in Arab weakness. The Europeans do not distinguish their position from that of the United States and Israel, as de Gaulle wanted them to do. This concurrence tends to snowball, because the spontaneous reaction of the Arab masses, Islamic manipulation, the disappearance of moderate Arab diplomacy, and such violent and ill-considered moves as those of Saddam Hussein, strengthen the anti-Arab voices in Europe. Under this state of affairs, the mediocrity of the

European vision works against its own interests, to the exclusive benefit of the United States and Israel.

Notes

1. Samir Amin, *Delinking* (London: Zed Books, 1990).

2. Amiya Bagchi, contribution to a collective work on the globalization of the third world, mimeographed (Dakar: Third World Forum, 1991).

3. See, for example, Suthy Prasartset, contribution to a collective work on the globalization of the third world, mimeographed (Dakar: Third World Forum, 1991).

4. Yoshikara Kunio, *The Rise of Ersatz Capitalism in Southeast Asia* (Manila: Manila University Press, 1988).

5. See Alain Joxe, *Le cycle de la dissuasion 1945-1990* (Paris: La Découverte, 1990), for a discussion of this cycle.

3
THE CRISIS OF SOCIALISM

The collapse of the Communist regimes of Europe that began in the fall of 1989 was a real turning point in history. Although it was astonishingly rapid, this collapse had been brewing since the Twentieth Party Congress in 1956. In fact, this accelerated reconstruction of the world system was preceded by a dismantling of the beginnings of autonomous development in the third world, which had flourished in the favorable climate from 1955 to 1975. The offensive of the ultra-liberal right had been so successful by then that social democrats (predominant in the Western left) had decided they must rally to liberalism. Triumphant liberal ideology proclaimed the end of socialism.

In the wake of these events today, to debate socialism one must start again from its foundations—the theses of bourgeois liberalism and the critiques that socialism has made of them—to examine the problems of the principal regions of the world (East, West, South), their common problems, and the strategies of a progressive response.

Overall, liberalism defines itself with three axioms:

First axiom of liberalism: The "market" represents economic rationality *per se*, outside any specific social context. Without the market, there can be only chaos.

This erroneous postulate expresses the economistic alienation essential for capitalist legitimacy, nothing more. The market does not in fact rationalize social relations. On the contrary, the framework of social relations determines how the market will operate. From an alienated, economistic standpoint, economic laws are analogous to laws of nature and exert external forces on every human action, and the economy is the product of innate social behavior. There is no economic rationality *per se*, but merely the expression of the demands of a social system at the level of economic management.

But no such social system is rational from a humanist point of view if it fails to meet the needs of the human beings subject to it. Unemployment, polarization in world development, and ecological waste are manifestations of the irrationality of this system, *really existing capitalism*. These negative phenomena are, purely and simply, necessary products of the market. The rationality of the market reproduces the irrationalities of the social system.

Second axiom of liberalism: Democracy equals capitalism. Without capitalism, there can be no democracy. This is mere trickery. Contemporary opinion, broadly typified by Anglo-American evolutionism, impoverishes the debate by treating democracy as a set of narrowly defined rights and practices, independent of the desired social result. This brand of democracy can then stabilize the society by leaving the "evolution" to "objective forces." The latter are in the last resort governed by science and technology, operating independently of the human will. Hence the functional role of the revolutionary process in history can be played down.

Socialist thought lies poles apart from this line of argument. The analysis of economistic alienation provided by Marx, central to any scientific and realistic understanding of capitalist reproduction, rehabilitates the crucial function of revolutions as moments of qualitative transformation and the crystallization of potentialities inconceivable without them.

In each of the three great revolutions of the modern world (the French, Russian, and Chinese), the play of ideas and social forces at moments of radicalization succeeded in moving far beyond the requirements of historical, necessary social transformation. Hence Jacobin democracy did more than merely establish bourgeois power. Although the Jacobins conceived of democracy in a framework of private ownership, their intention to establish power genuinely at the service of the people clashed with the needs of the bourgeoisie. At this stage of social development, the bourgeoisie looked for little more than a qualified democracy, such as occurred elsewhere in the nineteenth century. They were also willing to compromise with the monarchy and the aristocracy. The aspirations of the people—the crowd of peasants and artisans—went further. They wanted something more than free trade, to such an extent that during the convention, they launched the astonishingly modern slogan, "Liberalism is the enemy of democracy!" This was a foretaste of a socialist consciousness yet to come.

In the same way, the USSR in the 1920s and China in the Maoist period both expressed a Communist vision well beyond the requirements of the national and popular reform on the agenda. Certainly these moments of radicalization are fragile. In the end, narrower concepts more consonant with "objective" needs win the day. But it would be quite wrong to underestimate their significance as an indication of the way the movement is bound to continue.

Bourgeois democracy is the product of the revolution that dethroned "tributary metaphysics."[1] It establishes equal rights and personal liberties, but not equality, except under the law. As late as the latter half of the nineteenth century, the labor movement could impose unqualified political democracy and seize social rights, but only in the framework of a compromise based on acceptance of capitalist management of the economy and made possible by world polarization to the benefit of the industrial centers. Western democracy is thereby restricted to the political domain, while economic management continues to be based on nondemocratic principles of private ownership and competition. The capitalist mode of production does not of itself *require* democracy, but its characteristic oppression is *in fact hidden* in economic alienation. By contrast, the socialist project of a classless society, free of economic alienation, *implies* a democratic structure. Once capitalist reliance on competition is broken, social relations based on cooperation among workers, and not on their subjugation, are inconceivable without a full flowering of democracy.

If what are known as the third world countries have rarely seen their political systems operate in a genuinely democratic form, this is not a hangover from some traditional culture. What I call really existing capitalism, that is, *capitalism as a world system and not as a mode of production*, taken at its highest level of abstraction, has until now always generated polarization on a world scale. Unfortunately, this dimension has always been underestimated in socialist thought, including Marxism. The international polarization inherent in this expansion in turn brings a manifold internal polarization: growing inequality in income, widespread unemployment, marginalization, and the like. Seeing the world system as the only ultimately meaningful unit of analysis is crucial to understanding what is at stake in its struggles, namely that the essential reserve army of capitalism is to be found at the periphery of the system.

Hence instability is the rule in the political life of the peripheral nations. The political norm of the vicious dictatorship (whether military or not), broadly amenable to the expansion of world capital, is occasionally shaken by explosions, which rarely lead to real political democracy. The most common response is the populist model. Such regimes genuinely address at least some aspects of the social problem and try to develop strategies to reduce the tragic consequences of peripheralization, but they do not break with capitalism.

Between the right-wing dictatorships and the popular movements there is a middle ground onto which "petty democracy" can sometimes sneak. Such regimes recognize the principle of multi-party elections and grant a measure of free speech, but fall short of addressing fundamental social problems and/or challenging relations of dependence and subjugation to the world system. These "democracies" are little more than expressions of the crisis of the despotic system of capitalism. Latin America, Korea, and the Philippines provide examples of contradictions unresolved by such regimes. Democracy imposed in such circumstances faces a striking dilemma: either the democratic political system surrenders to the demands of world "adjustment" and, because it then cannot consider any substantial social reforms, the democracy soon reaches crisis (as in Argentina). Or, the popular forces take charge of the democracy and impose the reforms. But the political system then comes quickly into conflict with world capitalism and must shift from its national bourgeois project to a national and popular project.

The areas of the periphery most affected by capitalist expansion are in a more desperate plight. The historical record of capitalist expansion must own up to much more than the "development" it has engendered. Actually existing capitalism has a destructive side that is invariably omitted from its flattering self-portraits. Here, the usual pattern of power is the Duvaliers in Haiti, the Somozas in Nicaragua, and a disturbing number of dictatorships of the same stamp in contemporary Africa.

Third axiom of liberalism: A wide open door to the world system is the *sine qua non* of development. Without free trade, therefore, there can be no development. The underlying hypothesis is that although development necessarily depends to an important extent on internal circumstances peculiar to each society, integration into the world economy is necessary if a country is to develop its resources. Often, this axiom is surreptitiously replaced by another, far stronger one, which claims that the open door is sufficient: with free trade there will necessarily be development. This thesis is not only contradicted by the history of five centuries of capitalist expansion—five centuries of incessant polarization reproduced and intensified up to the present and into the foreseeable future. But the thesis is also scientifically unsound, even by the standards of liberal thought. The "world market" in question is truncated, and restricted to goods and capital; despite international migrations, there has never been any suggestion of a "world labor market," and no prospect of one. Liberal economic theory demonstrates that maintaining the mobility of a single factor of production, capital, while two other factors, labor and natural resources, are imprisoned by natural and political geography, cannot lead to uniform world productivity and social conditions.

Under such circumstances, the worldwide law of value can only produce and reproduce polarization. In this sense, integration into the world system is by nature unfavorable and becomes increasingly so. I have argued this thesis on intuitive evidence. A few decades were enough to allow nineteenth century Germany to "catch up" to England. How long would Brazil need to catch up to the United States?

Undoubtedly, the forms and content of the polarization have evolved over time. From the Industrial Revolution to World War II, there was a distinct difference between industrialized and nonindustrialized countries. Accelerated industrialization of some areas of the third world does not, in my view, raise a question mark over polarization as such, but merely over its forms. The mechanisms of the new polarization are founded on various forms of domination: financial (new forms of worldwide finance capital); technological (in relationship to the new scientific and technological revolution); cultural (with the growing influence of the media); and military. In this context the newly industrializing countries are not semi-peripheral nations on the way to becoming new centers, but the true periphery of tomorrow.

By contrast, the countries of the so-called fourth world are not true peripheries, but are like the areas destroyed by capitalist expansion in its earlier forms. The parlous condition of the fourth world is not the outcome of a "refusal" to integrate within the international division of labor and a failed attempt to delink. In fact, the fourth world, which is spoken of as something new, has been a consistent feature of capitalist expansion. A clear but lamentable example of this pervasive phenomenon is provided by the areas of slave labor in the Americas in the period of mercantilism, Northeast Brazil and the West Indies (including Haiti). These areas were regarded as prosperous in their day; and they were the heart of the periphery corresponding to the system of the time. Later, new structures of capitalist development marginalized them, and they are today among the most grievously wretched parts of the third world. Is Africa not now on the road to exclusion from the world division of labor by a system that has consigned the continent to specialization in agriculture and mining until the soils are exhausted, and by a technological revolution that provides substitutes for some of its still-plentiful raw materials? Fourth world societies that have been rejected by the system cannot, by definition, solve their problems through open door policies.

From the standpoint of the various peoples of the earth, unification of the entire world system under the sway of the market is undesirable. It is not even the most likely outcome of the evolution now under way, so bitter are the conflicts provoked by the market in a world of Darwinism. The ideological discourse of the West, which has chosen this strategy, aims to conceal the bitterness of these conflicts.

Socialism has scientific justification, not merely moral justification, in rejecting the three liberal theses that say economic rationality requires the market, democracy requires capitalism, and development requires free trade. All currents of socialist thought go beyond the philosophy of the Enlightenment, which sought to establish a rational basis that would serve society for all time. Socialism instead comes from an analysis of the historical limits of the rationality in question, namely its capitalist form, and offers a qualitatively more advanced society, aiming at a more complete mastery over human destiny. Here again, the Marxist theory of alienation returns to center stage. The scientific and social project of socialism is to liberate humanity from alienation in its bourgeois economistic form. This agenda cannot be defined more precisely in advance. Although it is possible to be precise about what must be abolished (such as private ownership of the means of production), it is not possible—in the absence of concrete social praxis—to delineate new methods of socialist management in advance. Any attempt to do so would militate against the liberation project itself, whereby the responsibility for shaping destiny can lie only with the succeeding generations, who will make their own history.

This being the case, one can never insist enough, in my opinion, that the socialist critique of bourgeois postulates is mistaken about the importance of the polarization that the world expansion of capital produces. Partaking of the bourgeois optimism that claims capitalist globalization homogenizes human conditions on a planetary scale, this critique envisions a rapid passage, not to socialism, but to a universal classless communism, by way of a rapid socialist transformation. I do not hold it against the Western socialist movement that it has committed this blunder, a natural product of the surrounding conditions; I address the reproach to us, the socialists of the periphery, upon whom it is incumbent to get out of our Eurocentric rut. But it is necessary to know that the Russian Communists, and behind them the Communists of China and the third world, share the weaknesses of this heritage. The essence of the present confusion comes from this heritage, in my opinion.

I shall not reopen the debate about the supposed utopianism of the final objective; I am one of those who think that adherence to humanist values requires a utopian vision. I shall say only that I do not conceive of the universal society as a paradise regained or a model achieved, much less a model already built in this place or that. No more than capitalism can such a society be "the end of history." I conceive, therefore, that the fight for the values it represents will remain a struggle without end. Progress in this direction will remain forever relative, as in the quest for scientific knowledge.

The Collapse of Eastern Europe: The End of Socialism?

We are still faced with the fact that the so-called socialist societies of the East abolished private ownership and established self-styled socialist systems of economic and political management. *These systems, particularly those in Europe, have collapsed.* Must we conclude that the socialist project itself is hopelessly utopian?

If we want to provoke a fruitful debate on these experiences, we must turn to the character of the so-called socialist revolutions in the East and the historical limits of the capitalism from which they emerged. Two approaches are possible. One can focus on what defines capitalism at its highest level of abstraction—namely, the contradiction between capital and labor. This viewpoint inevitably leads to a vision of the evolution of society. The backward (peripheral) capitalist societies must "catch up" with the advanced societies before they are in turn faced with the challenges of a possible (or perhaps necessary) supersession of the limits of those advanced societies. Or one may place more emphasis on the traits of really existing capitalism, which in its actual worldwide expansion has given rise to a center/periphery polarization impossible to overcome within the framework of capitalism itself. Nearly all currents of socialist thought have underestimated this dimension of capitalism, as I have said.

A challenge to the capitalist order on the basis of revolts on its periphery requires a serious rethinking of the issue of the "transition to socialism" and the abolition of classes. The Marxist tradition, however subtly interpreted, is handicapped by an initial theoretical vision of *worker* revolutions, on the basis of advanced forces of production, initiating a fairly speedy transition and marked by democratic power for the mass of the people. This is power that is more democratic in principle than that of the most democratic of the bourgeois states. By contrast, I would suggest that the profoundly unequal character inherent in capitalist expansion has brought onto history's agenda a revolution by people of the periphery. This revolution is anticapitalist, in the sense that it stands up against really existing capitalist development that has become unbearable. But for all that, it is not socialist, even though it rises up against capital in its cruelest manifestation. By force of circumstance it has a complex character.

These postcapitalist societies are now faced with the demand for substantial development of the forces of production. It is illusory to imagine basing an alternative development on poverty, even if one rejects the consumer lifestyle of capitalism in its advanced centers and takes into account its real waste and inhumanity.

Recognizing this does not mean accepting the thesis that an initial passage through a phase of capitalist accumulation is inevitable. Such a bourgeois revolution is a most unlikely outcome of a mass movement that is led by political parties with an openly anticapitalist ideology and view of the future. A capitalist expansion fostered by the local bourgeoisie but open to the world system will here be challenged by the mass of the people, for whom it could only be a form of oppression.

This specific and new contradiction, not envisaged in Marx's classic concept of the socialist transition, gives the postcapitalist regimes their real quality, of a national and popular construct. Under this construct there is a conflicting mix of aspirations and achievements of a socialist kind and aspirations of a capitalist kind called for by the need to develop the forces of production.

This contradiction, inherent in the long transition imposed by the unequal development of capitalism, can obviously be defined by three fundamental elements. These are the inverse counterparts of the three liberal axioms criticized above: bureaucratic planning (rationality without the market); anti-democratic political monopoly of a ruling party-state (no democracy and no capitalism); and total delinking from the capitalist world system, almost to the point of autarky (development with a closed door). This last has been more an imposition by the West than a desire on the part of the East.

It is certainly significant that this so-called socialist construct has worked through a nondemocratic political system and bureaucratic planning. The complex explanation includes social and cultural-historical determinants and the limits of the ideologies of the countries' revolutionary intelligentsia—Leninism and Maoism. I believe that national and popular hegemony could operate differently from the way they have operated in the past, that there is room for political democracy and market forces. These, after all, cannot operate in socialist societies any more than in capitalist ones outside the boundaries of the social base on which they rest. Indeed, I would go further and say that for this national and popular hegemony to progress, it must move in these directions.

Under these circumstances, the magnitude of the crisis of the societies of the East should come as no surprise, even if like everyone else we have been astounded by the suddenness with which it has manifested itself. These societies now face a triad of options that I briefly summarize as follows:

1. Evolution toward a bourgeois democracy, *or* progress beyond it, by strengthening the social power of the workers in the management of the economy.

2. Restoration of an out-and-out market economy, *or* progress through a carefully controlled resort to market forces guided by democratic planning.

3. An unguarded door open wide to the exterior, *or* guarded relations with the surrounding world, albeit directed toward increased trade.

The confused theoretical debates and political disputes that are sending shudders down spines in the East arise in part because the ideological label "socialist" has imparted confusion as to the nature of the genuinely national and popular revolutions that established some of the regimes in question. But more pertinent is the fact that the conflicting forces of capitalism and socialism are meeting within genuine national struggles. The forces anxious to restore capitalism propose unilateral acceptance of the market as a springboard for the restoration of private ownership, and of an open door, with or without democracy in the Western sense, according to the tactical requirements of their project. If the socialist forces dither in their resistance to this project, if they find it difficult to articulate a coherent alternative along the lines sketched above, it is because the lack of democratic debate and the ideological confusion over the status of the evolving governments have proved to be major impediments to action. Need I add that the Western ideological offensive, orchestrated through powerful media, is massing entirely on the side of the pro-capitalist (and anti-democratic) forces?

A political response to the three options posed above would lead to intensive internal class struggle, already (silently) under way. A significant minority in the East—perhaps 20 percent—might benefit from the restoration of capitalism. But in light of the inadequate levels of development and international competitiveness achieved by the socialist countries, this minority could never attain the Western standard of living that fuels their aspirations without grinding down the mass of the people.

In this struggle, the people of the various countries of the East start with unequal weapons. Intuitively, one can grasp why those who have by force made their own socialist, nationalist, and popular revolutions (the USSR, China, Yugoslavia, etc.) have an ideological weapon that enables them to put a progressive complexion on their struggles. By contrast, those of the Eastern European countries, with no comparable historical achievement, run the risk of being bewitched by the attraction of annexing themselves to Western Europe. In the current crisis, assertions such as "recourse to the market" and "an open door to the exterior" remain ambiguous because they unite those who seek a launching pad to capitalism and those who seek a progressive social approach to the political and economic management of their society, and thus a genuine social advance. It is interesting to note that social surveys in the USSR show that the privileged classes prefer the pluralist democracy and a market open to the exterior formula, whereas the popular classes remain attached to the achievements of socialism (full employment, social services, national independence, and public ownership). The latter favor planning, along with democratization of the political system. Gorbachev apparently straddled these antinomian currents, allied only in their opposition to the conservatives, who have always hoped for a standstill. One notes similar cleavages in Yugoslavia.

Are Eastern Europe and the USSR incurably doomed to a third world transformation, hence to be compradorized?

Will they surrender to the demands of unmitigated transnationalization, which would consign them to a third world
fate? Or, as liberal ideology argues, will capitalism rescue
them from the impasse of "socialism" and grant them rapid
development along the lines of Western European countries?

Things being what they are, the countries of Eastern Europe will have difficulty avoiding the calamity for their
working classes that will result from integration into the
capitalist system as it is. The integrated national structures
established over the past forty years are already being dis-
mantled to the benefit of expansion of foreign capital (German first of all, but also European, Japanese, and American).
The new local bourgeoisie will pay for their economic bene-
fits by having to accept comprador status. They may find
social support in other classes of intermediate strata—rich
peasants or petty entrepreneurs—as is the case in the third
world. The ordinary people will pay for these "adjustments"
by a drastic cut in their standard of living, widespread unemployment, and cuts in social services. Nor is this a "brief
transitional period," as their new leaders would have them
believe, but once and for all.

It is quite obvious to an expert from the World Bank that
the Polish problem is very simple. Wages must be cut in half
(without regard for the impact of this measure on productivity) and an unemployment level of two or three million
accepted. The situation, remarkably similar to that of Argentina, is obscured by the illusions of the Polish people, who
have never understood that in the world system they wish
to join, their place is closer to that of the industrializing
countries of the third world than to the Western societies
whose democracy they admire. The Polish people must also
be wary of a drift from transitional democracy to an author-
itarian regime (based on the Catholic church, like that of

General Józef Pilsudski) as the only regime capable of impos-
ing the "discipline" that capitalism demands. Evolution of
this kind is also to be feared in other historically Catholic
nations as well. Potentially troublesome reactions must be
expected, fueling secondary nationalisms (which do not
challenge Western domination). These then become the
bases for "populist" dictatorships such as these countries
experienced in the 1920s, 1930s, and 1940s.

The USSR is a more complex example. The character of the
social conflicts under way and the perception of what is at
stake —the country's role as a military superpower and the
acuteness of the resulting national questions—have occurred
so fast as to outstrip the best informed studies. We are left
with the almost intuitive thought that the former USSR,
should it find renewal—or the Russian heartland, high-
lighted in the wake of the Soviet Union's breakup— may
achieve a subtle combination of democratic political reform,
better economic management, greater integration in the
world economy, and at the same time continuity and reinforcement of its national structure. The social character of this
positive compromise between the demands of transnationalization and the creation of internal autonomy will be
close to what I have described as "a national and popular
social front"—produced by the 1917 revolution but lost in the
ideology of so-called socialist construction. This optimistic
scenario does not stop there; such a system would inevitably
evolve toward a developed capitalist pole or toward a system
with more progressive social content.

It goes without saying, however, that this optimistic hypothesis is far from the only one possible. For whatever the
facts, the evolution of the world will not take form until it has
emerged from the present chaos. This chaos, which threatens
to last, can only resolve itself through a historical retreat from

which recovery will be difficult. If the illusions of "the market" and "the West" should dominate all other considerations, the risk of third-worldization of the USSR cannot be dismissed. The country will revert to the condition of Russia before 1914, backward and subaltern. In addition, should the Russians insist they are "Europeans," the peoples of the Caucasus and Central Asia will feel they have no political affinity with the reformed union.

Generally speaking, one is struck by the political näiveté that has grown up among the people of the nondemocratic regimes of Eastern Europe. Their attacks on the *nomenklatura*, intended as an indictment of privilege under actually existing socialism, ignore the fact that the class aspiring to form a bourgeoisie will inevitably be composed of just this *nomenklatura*, and that the privileges it has enjoyed are nothing in comparison with the social inequalities of actually existing capitalism.

The initiative for change in the East has in fact been taken by the ruling class itself. This is constituted on the basis of a statism that has been the way of dealing with the capitalism/socialism contradiction within the national and popular construct. The ruling class hopes now to be rid of the constraints of the popular classes and to opt four-square for capitalism. The scuttling of the system to which this ruling class now directs itself, so astonishing to Western commentators, is not really surprising at all: it is the logical terminus of its evolution, and was foreseen by Mao. This class, in attacking its own system, repeats all the outworn prejudices of the bourgeois critique of socialism but refrains from pointing out that the system it is abandoning has been marvelously effective in making possible its own constitution as a bourgeoisie.

The case of China is somehow specific and different. That said, the analysis must be taken further, with emphasis on the character of the changes after the death of Mao Zedong and the problems they raise for the future. I should say in this regard, and as a further contradiction to the fashionable critics of Maoism, that economic growth in the successive Maoist periods was stronger and better balanced in the long term, thanks to a constant effort at collective investment in irrigation, reforestation, and the like. It is understood that the acceleration in agricultural growth allowed under Deng Xiaoping's new policy produced apparently brilliant results during the first half of the 1980s, but with no future, since it was to the detriment of the bases for long-term growth. Similarly, industrial acceleration was focused on the coastal regions. Conversely, the Maoist strategy could not be sustained indefinitely and had reached a plateau by the end of the 1970s. But Deng's later choices provoked contradictions of all kinds, whose resolution is subject to the open and concealed conflicts now under way. One of these contradictions is the premature acceleration of urbanization.

As we know, Deng opted for an open door to both internal and external capitalism, an option, it should be remembered, eagerly supported by the West. The democracy movement has (remarkably) recruited forces both from the well-off classes, who openly hope to restore capitalism, and from the majority (some claiming to be Maoist), who complain they have been harmed by capitalist developments during the Deng era. The Western media, who describe repression of the democracy movement as a return to "Maoism" mixed with "Stalinism," have certainly not contributed to clarity. Instead, they have played a leading role in supporting the reactionary option of restoring capitalism, even if it must be carried out to the total detriment of democracy.

The Third World Remains the Zone of Tempests

The question of the future of socialism is not limited to possible advances or retreats on the part of the countries of the East. One must look also at the countries of the third and fourth worlds—true peripheries and societies destroyed by capitalist expansion, where development that can meet the material needs of all social strata is impossible within the framework of capitalism, and where it becomes necessary to consider alternative development outside capital's bounds. This is the meaning of the expression *delinking*. It is not a recipe, but a fundamental and principled choice—to divorce the criteria of rationality in economic life from those that govern world capitalism, breaking out of the constraints of world-capitalist value, and substituting a law of value of national popular reference.

If the bourgeoisie are incapable of delinking, and if only a popular alliance can be persuaded that this is required for any development worthy of the name, the social dynamism must lead in a direction that we can only describe as socialist. It is clear that the socialism in question remains a prospect for society well into the future, and not a ready-made model.

The current changes in the world economy and political and cultural situation cannot alter the polarizing character of really existing capitalism, but can only heighten the contradictions through which it is expressed. The policies of surrender to world unification through the market—described as "adjustment" for the periphery countries, although one speaks of "restructuring" where the centers are concerned—do not neutralize its effects. Such policies are not therefore acceptable alternatives to a national, popular "breaking away," which is necessary now more than ever. The national bourgeoisie of the third world, who have co-opted national liberation to their own advantage, have already become compradors, under the laws of evolution of the world system. They are therefore incapable of mediating the new worldwide phenomena to the advantage of their own countries. The popular classes are still confused and indecisive following the exhaustion of the former national liberation movements. Hence it is difficult to forecast the next step in an uninterrupted popular revolution that still threatens upheavals in the peripheries of the global states.

In the short term, the responses of the third world are generally inadequate, as in the past. The revival of fundamentalist religious movements here and there is itself a symptom of the crisis, and not an adequate response to its challenge.

New Trends in the West?

If the transnational globalization option is clearly accepted in the West by both the electoral left and right, the reason is that whatever path is chosen will not bring a dramatic social impact. A particular choice—such as a European common market without political and social harmonization—could marginalize the poor periphery of Europe, bringing widespread unemployment and decline in Spanish Asturias and Greece, for example. But Europe as a political entity can withstand these setbacks, turn the Mediterranean shores into playgrounds for the Northern Europeans, and absorb the immigrant workers from the area.

Yet there is no reason, of course, to exclude the West from the debate on the prospects for socialism. One must neither discount a labor movement that has made possible the achievements of social democracy nor overlook the democratic victories of the West. But standing still means falling back. Socialist advance in the West requires that the people free themselves from alienation and idolatry as they appear in societies whose major means of communication are all in the hands of the dominant classes. The intense communication campaign that operates within really existing capitalism does nothing to contribute to liberation or democratization. Quite the contrary. People who are not permanent residents of the West on a day-to-day basis are always struck by the incredible saturation by the dominant media—a veritable carpet bombing of the public consciousness. From one country to another, from liberals and conservatives to socialists, an ideological consensus forces near-unanimity on many of the central issues. The pluralism that is so vaunted as synonymous with democracy is stripped of all real content, and minor, provincial differences among competitors of the political class are blown up to bizarre proportions. At a time when "the end of ideology" is being proclaimed, the West has never before been so subject to so exclusively ideological a discourse.

In a reference elsewhere to the remarkable breakthroughs in social consciousness exemplified by the women's movement, I deemed it necessary to express reservations on the real *extent* of these breakthroughs. They can be *absorbed* by a system that remains basically capitalist and imperialist in its relations with the periphery, or, on the contrary, become nodes of positive change. Everything, in the end, depends on how the people of Western Europe, the United States, and Japan see their competition with one another, and how they see East-West and North-South relations.

In any case, the choice of globalization pushes on the West with all its negative weight. Under these conditions, the geopolitical dimension of problems takes on particular importance, not in the sense that nations constitute the only active subjects of history, but in the sense that geopolitics defines the framework of social struggles and politics, and assigns to their different possible outcomes probabilities that are more or less favorable.

Besides, until now the Europe of the EC has constituted the geopolitical framework of an intensification of globalization accepted by a wide range of public opinion. One will notice, nonetheless, that in this framework the European left has failed at what would seem to be its role: combatting the prevalent viewpoint of the right (the "common market for capital") and prescribing a social Europe. The rallying of social democrats to the theses of liberalism underscored this failure. Their utter lack of audacity, to borrow a phrase of Alain Lipietz, does not bode well for the near term.[2]

The first challenge had not yet been raised (and would it ever?) when a new series of challenges concerning the structure of the EC appeared. Under such conditions, the future of socialism in Western Europe largely will depend on the evolution of new intra-European relations. Without a doubt, the ideological bipolarization stemming from the socialist revolutions starting in 1917 will be erased if capitalism is restored in the East. An evolution of this sort, which is unfortunately what a large part of the Western anticommunist left is calling for, will eventuate in a long-lasting setback for socialist aspirations in Europe. It cannot in any way help the cause of social democracy, but as a matter of course will redound to the benefit of the right. In contrast, a deepening of national, popular movements would contribute to the renewal of socialist conscience in the countries of the East. This is the possibility most favorable to the cause of socialism, but it has been rejected by the Western European left.

Without doubt, the central axis along which the future of socialism in the West will be decided is that of North and South. This is nothing new to anyone who understands that the determining dimension in history is that which structures the world expansion of capital. The sharpness of the East-West conflict certainly eclipsed this fact for a time, just as the inter-imperialist conflict occupied center stage in the years leading up to 1914. The intensification of intra-Western and East-West conflicts accompanied therefore a renewal of hostility toward those who are the principal victims of capitalist expansion, in Asia, Africa, and Latin America. Many signs point to this regression today; among them, the resurgence of racism and colonialist arrogance seen in the reconversion of NATO bases, whose weapons are now trained on the south shore of the Mediterranean.

How may one hope, under these conditions, for a progressive breakthrough in the West? In the strong sense of the term, social progress entails an evolution toward the hegemony of the salaried class, to recall once more the thesis of Alain Lipietz, with which I agree completely. We certainly are not heading in that direction now, and the idea is as foreign to social democracy as secularism is to Islam. When will we head in this direction if the dominant concept of North-South relations is not simultaneously challenged? This critique that Maoism addressed in its day to the Soviet Union could then take on a redoubled vigor. For, in contrast to the tentative Soviet imperialism—tempered by the intrinsic weaknesses of the system and its ideological tradition of internationalism, at least at the level of rhetoric—that of the West is more efficacious, follows a Eurocentric (racist) tradition, and is infinitely more dangerous to the future of humanity. Are there not already signs pointing in this direction? The elegy that Lipietz intoned for the German syndicates (which he said were headed in the direction of the hegemony of the salaried) calls forth some positive reservations on my part. I see the beginning of the social-imperialist evolution. Will not Germany's retreat from the European project also go in this direction?

Socialism or Barbarism?

The contours of a new globalization of capital remain vague. The configuration that materializes will result from conflicts that will be inevitable despite the liberalism common to the nations of the capitalist center. Meanwhile, according to the absurd hypothesis that the national and social forces in dispute will agree to sacrifice their several interests to the strict logic of globalization by the market, the reshaped world will be formidable. Hence the future remains open to various possibilities, and there is no justification for abandoning the struggle to promote a better world. This is no plea for voluntarism, since the political options that limit the possible futures are historically objective. Exploring these options calls for examining alternatives along three axes of evolution: (1) the center-periphery contradiction, governed by the logic of world capitalism; (2) East-West relations; and (3) intra-Western competition. I have attempted to explore these options briefly, from the starting point of unilateral unification by the market that constitutes the essence of the Western project.

More than ever, the forces of the left have a duty to promote a credible alternative to this disastrous option. I shall briefly review the possible features of this alternative.

First, the only meaningful strategy for the progressive forces on a world scale—on whose basis the peoples of the

West, East, and South could together draw new breath—must envision a polycentric world. The various components must be articulated in a flexible way, allowing for political, economic, and cultural diversity. It must be acknowledged at the outset that the problems the people of the world must solve differ from one area to another. It is therefore essential that the world system permit each group the autonomy to promote its own interests. There must be balance between general interdependence and this legitimate concern for autonomy. The logic of mutual and reciprocal adjustment must be substituted for unilateral "adjustment" by the weakest, and expansion for the exclusive benefit of the strongest.

Second, polycentrism means that the countries of the East and South must pursue development policies that are delinked in the sense I have given to this word. This strategy looks to advances toward socialism (democratization and the strengthening of national and popular trends) and not to a restoration of capitalism in the countries of the East; it also looks to a refusal by the countries of the South to become compradors. It must likewise allow progressive advances in the countries of the West, through the opening of nonmarket social spaces and through other reforms based on socialization of economic management.

Third, with particular reference to the third world, this strategy favors progress in the organization of the productive forces even to the detriment of international competitiveness. It places high on the agenda an agricultural revolution marked by maximum equality, and transformation of the informal sector into a popularly managed transitional economy. It calls for an effective combination of planning and market forces as the foundation for economic and social democracy. The vision of polycentrism it inspires gives the countries and regions of the third world a measure of autonomy denied them under world unification by the market.

Fourth, as regards international cooperation for interdependence, the strategy aims to encourage an embryo of a democratic world government and, for example, a world tax to be spent on environmental measures. It also aims to reduce the arms race, notably by the superpowers. It aims finally to breathe new life into the democratic institutionalization of world management through the UN.

Let me say in conclusion that the construction of a polycentric world with new prospects for socialism implies acute awareness of the cultural universalism of humanity's project. On this point I have put forward elsewhere a critique of the Eurocentrism and cultural nationalism that form the obverse image.[3]

Notes

1. Samir Amin, *Eurocentrism* (New York: Monthly Review Press, 1989), pp. 15-59.

2. Alain Lipietz, *Choisir l'audace* (Paris: La Découverte, 1989).

3. Amin, *Eurocentrism*, pp. 124-52.

4
THE DEMOCRATIC CHALLENGE

The recent past has shown a global trend toward the democratization of political regimes that may well be irreversible. In the socialist countries at least the trend has been forced on the powers that be; they must adapt to its demands or perish. In third world capitalist countries the call for democracy has not reached the same degree of intensity; it is frequently limited to the middle classes and organized elements in the urban popular classes, such as the unions. Even so, it signals the permeation of democratic consciousness throughout the political system of much of the third world.

This trend has appeared concomitantly with another generalized offensive for the liberation of market forces, aimed at establishing the domination of private property, legitimating social inequalities, and reducing statism of all kinds. The coincidence of these two trends makes ours an era of intense ideological confusion. The "market"—a euphemism for capitalism—is regarded as the central axis of any development. Openness to the world market and the adoption of an internal system subservient to it is the order of the day. Democracy is regarded as the necessary and natural product of submission to this order. The concept of democracy that is extolled in this liberal offensive is impoverished by an evolutionist fixation that denies the historical importance of revolutionary processes. Revolutions, it is claimed, have never done any good; they entail too much violence to accomplish what would have evolved in their absence. The triumph of democracy and the market will mark "the end of history."

In the final analysis, we can only debate these beliefs by referring to the philosophical concepts underlying democracy's various meanings.

The contemporary world and the perceptions of where it is going are the products of the French, Russian, and Chinese revolutions, the three signal events of modern history. Echoing Immanual Wallerstein, I attach particular significance to the historical break announced by the French Revolution, which substituted secular legitimation of political and social action for the religious legitimation of what I have called tributary ideologies.[1] In that sense the French Revolution was the precondition for all later evolutions, whether of bourgeois democracy or socialism. The Paris Commune's slogan in 1871—"Neither God, nor Caesar, nor Tribune"— flowed from, and was an extension of, the "Liberty, Equality, Fraternity"of 1789.

My emphasis on this ideological outcome of the class wars of France is meant to challenge a certain conventional view of the relation of class struggle to the French Revolution. It was not on the French bourgeoisie's agenda to resolve the struggle between lord and landless peasant by overthrowing feudalism in favor of an egalitarian peasant society. This was the aim of the struggling peasants. The bourgeois project was the establishment of a system of exploitation these peasants never imagined. Capitalist society and the bourgeoisie developed on the fringes and in the interstices of feudal society, in the free towns, partly even among the peasantry. And it ripened slowly within social and political systems that were essentially feudal. The bourgeois political revolution then constituted the abolition of the *ancien régime* and the installation of a new regime dominated by the class newly dominant in the economy. The bourgeois revolution is not the starting point of the development of capitalism, but its culmination.

Such a coincidence between a peasant social revolution and a bourgeois political revolution has occurred only once in history, in the French Revolution, which was the sole genuine revolution of the bourgeois stage of history. The bourgeoisie were forced into the alliance, but it was *their* revolution. Their atypical advances and retreats then shaped the stages of the revolution itself and determined its later evolution. There is no comparable coincidence, not even in England. There, the peasant-bourgeois revolution of the mid-seventeenth century expressed its politics in religious reinterpretation (whereas the French Revolution made politics secular). The English event was soon aborted, and the so-called Glorious Revolution that came later was hardly a revolution at all. Nor was the North American rebellion comparable. Liberation from the colonial yoke was a political separation without revolutionary implications; it merely confirmed the power of the merchants, independent farmers, and plantation owners who had already established themselves under the loose hegemony of Britain. It is also significant that the American Revolution did not raise the issue of slavery.

The general rule, then, is that capitalism is established without a peasant revolution, even when peasant struggles shape its course and contribute to its outcome. But capitalism cannot develop without an "agricultural revolution," in the sense of establishing a propertied class that drives the surplus population from the land to modernize into production for the market. In all such cases the bourgeoisie attacks and seizes the state, then changes society from above.

The very special circumstances of the French Revolution explain its advances beyond the mere adjustment of the relation of production to the demands of capitalist development: its secularized legitimation, its universal concepts, its proclamation of the abolition of human subservience. These advances opened a window on a future yet to come. Without the French Revolution, utopian socialism and Marx would be unthinkable.

The Russian and Chinese revolutions also had a dimension of grandeur that is sometimes described as "messianic." This is wrong in my view, since the future they promised remains a realistic possibility, and a necessity if humankind is to avoid barbarism. Clearly, these advances, going even further than those conceived in Paris in 1793 and 1871 (since the phenomena of capitalism on the one hand and Marx on the other had occurred in the interim), are not the simple product of the objective demands for immediate social transformation advanced in Russia in 1917 and China in 1949.

I contend therefore that the three revolutions under discussion are the great moments when our vision of the modern world and its possible and desirable future was defined. To find earlier moments that were as decisive, we must go back 1,500 to 2,500 years to the great ideological revolutions that crystallized tributary society, expressed in our part of the world as Hellenism, Christianity, and Islam, and elsewhere in such forms as Confucianism and Buddhism. At the level of ideology, a dominant dimension of precapitalist society, such qualitative transformations were as gigantic as those that the three modern revolutions wrought in our era. These revolutions went beyond any mere adjustment to the demands of social evolution by proclaiming universalisms that the regional tributary societies did not require.[2]

The changes that have occurred between these revolutions have been of local and minor significance, manifesting the process of continual adjustment of the various social spheres to the constraints of evolution. Democracy, then, becomes a destabilizer, the means by which concepts "ahead of their time" continue to develop and encourage social action to progress.

The conventional theoretical explanation of the absence of democracy in the third world is meanwhile hollow. In a sequence of guises fashioned by shifts in intellectual fashion, these theories formulate and reformulate the paradigm of modernization: third world societies are half-traditional, half-modern, on the path to modernization, and still under the sway of the autocratic concept of power. They are also constrained by force of circumstance to democratize gradually in step with their attempt to catch up with the modern world. In this context, as in all others, the capitalist road is the only conceivable one, and leads inexorably to democratization.

This thesis, obscured during the 1960s by the popularity of "third-worldism" among Westerners, has made its latest appearance in a Weberian formulation.[3] Weber, as we know, distinguished supposedly traditional forms of power, which he described as patrimonial, personalized, and contrary to the modern concept of law, from the bureaucratic and depersonalized form based on modern legal concepts.

In truth, Weber's thesis on this matter is very Germanic, in the sense that it extends the particular characteristics of

German history to the whole of humankind. Power in pre-capitalist societies was not, as a general rule, either person-alized or disrespectful of law. The exemplar of tributary society, China, carried impersonal power to the limit in its mandarin bureaucracy. In the time of the pharoahs, Thutmose III of Egypt's eighteenth dynasty wrote to his vizier Rekheret: "What he [the vizier] must do is to take the law into account...."[4] Undoubtedly, European feudalism from the barbarian invasions to the thirteenth or fourteenth century comes close to the Weberian model in respect to the personalization of power. But in fact the fragmentation of power under feudalism, a precondition for its personaliza-tion, merely illustrates the fact that feudalism is a peripheral variety of tributary system, and not the general form of the precapitalist tradition.[5] It can also be seen that power lost this personalized characteristic in the mercantilist Europe of the absolute monarchies. In fact, the royal bureaucracies were similar to those of other advanced tributary societies, as contemporary observers were quick to note.[6] The singular exception was Germany, which remained in the seigneurial form long after its neighbors had moved forward.

However, the principal aspect of tributary ideology is not paternalism, but metaphysical domination. This is true of all instances, whether Confucianism in China, Islam in the Khalifate, or the peripheral forms of feudalism. Furthermore, patrimonial systems in no way disregarded the law. In the advanced tributary systems there was state law governing the whole of social life, as evidenced, for example, by the *sharia* in Islamic countries. In the feudal peripheral systems, seigneurial power, even when personalized, was obliged to respect customary peasant rights.

Is Weber's concept of power mainly bureaucratic in its impact? Certainly not. Its bureaucratic character is only the form through which it works. Its essential content is bourgeois, produced by the operation of bourgeois democracy, with the distinct exception, once again, of Germany, where the weakness of the bourgeoisie empowered the "enlightened despot" until very recent times. Here, Marx outshines Weber in his analyses of this German uniqueness. Here too, Weber stretches a particular characteristic—certainly typical of Wilhelmine Germany but not of parliamentary England or France of the Third Republic—to the West as a whole.

Weber's imitators (such as Richard Sandbrook) have tried to apply this dubious thesis to explain specific characteristics of power in contemporary black Africa, where in fact personalization and disregard for law do seem to have marked a great many postcolonial systems. These writers merely attribute such characteristics to African tradition.

But is the thesis of patrimonial power valid for precolonial Africa? Undoubtedly there is a certain resemblance to feudal Europe. For precolonial black Africa was pre-tributary, still largely at the stage I call "communal,"[7] whereas feudal Europe preserved its communal forms from their origin in a barbarism that gave to their system its primitive and peripheral character. This analogy illustrates the significance of customary rights in the two cases in the absence of bureaucratic state law—with the difference, nonetheless, that the form of the church in Europe confirmed the metaphysical dominance which defined this stage. In Africa, by contrast, the ideology of kinship which is appropriate to the communal stage still dominates the systems of legitimation of power. This ideology looks very much like personalized power. But this is much less the case than might be thought, as the power must operate within a framework of customary law that acts as a brake on capricious behavior on the part of the "chiefs."

As I shall later show, contemporary authorities in Africa have little connection with this supposed legacy, which has long since been discredited, particularly by the slave trade. The supposed charisma has no roots in tradition. It is a modern phenomenon to which we shall return.

The neo-Weberian thesis is not the only expression of the broader form of modernization. Recall the Latin American *desarrollismo* of the 1950s and 1960s, which argued that industrialization and bourgeois modernization would themselves bring democratic change. Dictatorship was regarded as a hangover from a supposed precapitalist past. The fallacy of this ingenious line of argument has been shown by the facts. Industrialization and modernization in this bourgeois framework have merely produced modernized dictatorship and replaced old oligarchical and patriarchical systems with efficient and modern fascism. Peripheral development could take no other course, as it aggravated social inequalities.

Nor is the absence of democracy from the periphery a hangover from an earlier era, but an inevitable consequence of the expansion of really existing capitalism. The international polarization inherent in this expansion brings internal polarization: growing inequality in income, widespread unemployment, and marginalization. The world system as a whole is therefore the only intelligible unit for understanding what is at stake in the third world, because the essential reserve army of capital is located there. This labor reserve is, to be sure, composed of a staggering mass of unemployed and underemployed urban workers—many times the number in the West, and in crisis—but also large numbers of nonwage laborers destined to be expelled from their land or the informal economy in which they make their living. The integration of portions of this reserve into the active army occurs either through semi-industrialization of the peripheries or migration toward the centers. But it is always limited by the employment strategies of the center states, and is possible only for an infinitesimal fraction of the worldwide reserve army. Liberalism, which has never envisioned extending its program of liberalized exchange and capital flows to unlimited labor migration, remains therefore a truncated swindle.

Hence instability is the rule in the political life of the peripheries. The backdrop of dictatorship, broadly congenial to the expansion of capital, is occasionally shaken by explosions that challenge it, but such explosions rarely lead to any semblance of political democracy. They most commonly give rise to regimes that can be characterized as populist. Such regimes address at least some aspects of the social problem and embark on a development strategy able to reduce some of the tragic consequences of peripheralization. These regimes must be given credit for industrialization (mainly led by the state), nationalization of the sectors dominated by foreign capital, agrarian reforms, efforts (sometimes remarkable) in education and health, and social rights offering a degree of job protection.

The populist regimes have their historical limits, too. On the one hand, they clash with imperial domination simply because any socially progressive policy at the periphery is incompatible with the worldwide expansion of capital. But they cannot take this conflict to its logical conclusion—delinking. On the other hand, these regimes are not democratic. They have often been popular and, as we say, supported by the masses. Charismatic leadership is a common feature. But the masses are maintained in an amorphous, passive condition, mobilized for support but not allowed to organize as a force autonomous from the authorities. Such regimes arise in societies trapped in a familiar situation and marked by weak class formations. When they embark on a national and popular transformation, they are unable to carry it through. The inherent weakness of the populist system, abetted by external aggression, brings about its collapse and, usually, a return to dictatorship.

There is a middle ground between dictatorships of the right and popular movements which sustain a degree of petty democracy. What I mean is regimes that recognize the principles of multi-party elections and grant a measure of free speech, but fall short of addressing fundamental social problems and/or challenging relations of dependence and subjugation to the world system. The range here is broad enough to include seeming "democracies," where the authorities retain the means—most frequently by electoral fraud—to remain in power, and other regimes that actually bow to the outcome of polls.

These "democracies" are little more than an expression of the crisis of the despotic system usual to capitalism. Latin America, Korea, and the Philippines exemplify the unresolvable contradictions. The development plans of the dictatorships these regimes have succeeded have not yielded the intended results. The crisis has demonstrated the impossibility of the whole project, particularly "independence." This predicament, for some, legitimates the ensuing dictatorship.

A democratic system imposed under such circumstances faces an either-or dilemma. Either it surrenders to the demands of world adjustment and democracy soon reaches a crisis (as is already the case in Argentina). Or the popular forces take hold of the democracy and impose the reforms, putting the system into conflict with world capitalism and forcing a shift from the national bourgeois project to a national and popular project. The dilemma of Brazil and the Philippines falls within this contradiction. In Argentina it has already been seen how the electors, wearied by the impotence of former President Raul Alfonsin's democracy, returned of their own accord to the populist sirens, this time wearing the guise of fascists openly submissive to foreign dictates.

The areas of the periphery most affected by capitalist expansion are in an even more desperate plight. The parlous condition of the fourth world is not the outcome of a refusal to fit into the international division of labor. To the contrary, the fourth world is a constant feature of capitalist expansion. Clear examples of this fourth world are provided by the areas of slave labor in the Americas in the period of mercantilism—Northeast Brazil and the West Indies, including Haiti. These areas were regarded as prosperous in their day and were the heart of the periphery corresponding to the world system of the time.

Later, the course of capitalist development marginalized these areas, and they are today among the most grievously wretched parts of the third world. The history of capitalist expansion must cover not only the development it has engendered. Capitalism has a destructive side that is often left out of its self-portraits. Has not Africa been consigned to specialize in agriculture and mining until its soils are exhausted and technological change provides substitutes for the materials it produces? And does this not put it on the road to exclusion from the world division of labor? Fourth world societies that have been delinked through rejection cannot solve their problems by adopting open-door policies.

The thesis of patrimonial power criticized above was formulated to cover such African regimes. At a superficial level the description fits. Political relations—whether involving petty tyrants or heads of state—are highly personalized and conducted wholly without regard for notions of legality and rights, whether of property or person. There has been a strong temptation to blame this supposed "legacy" on African tradition. A trace of racism may underlie this insinuation. In fact there is no legacy that could produce the fourth world phenomenon.

Should the fourth world African states be called, as Nzongola-Ntalaja suggested, "kleptocracies,"[8] closer to the domains of the Mafia than to chiefdoms, which are mindful of traditional rights? I think not. Such states are modern and operational in their own way. How else could their authorities manage under fourth world conditions, which deprive the state of any legitimacy based on economic development? Not only do the peasantry, the working class, and the urban fringe have nothing to look forward to, and know it, but even the bourgeoisie lacks any possible role in development. All that remains is the direct exploitation of power as a means of personal enrichment, or its indirect exploitation through pseudo private economic activities whose profitability depends entirely on relations with the administration. Terror, corruption, and extreme personalization are therefore essential to the operation of the system. Charisma—so often spoken of—has no place here. It is not a matter of charismatic leaders who have won genuine popularity at decisive moments in history, as in the populist regimes, but of a pseudo charisma concocted by the media but incapable of fooling the public. Superficially, the petty bourgeoisie might be regarded as the social base of such systems, insofar as members of this class share power and benefit from the budget. When this is not simply an illusion, the association reveals a measure of fascism in the petty bourgeois strata. Their hopes have been dashed, and in their powerlessness—in the absence of a revolutionary intelligentsia offering an alternative—they take refuge in the worship of power.

What Kind of Democracy?

Nowadays, the main task of progressive forces in the periphery of the system is to assert the missing democratic component, not to displace the national and popular components of liberation but to reinforce them. In fact, the old paradigm of national liberation largely ignored the democratic component essential for the pursuit of national and popular advance. Democratic consciousness may well be a new phenomenon. In the past, democratic demands were limited to particular segments of the urban bourgeoisie and were not vigorously expressed except during the radicalization of the anti-imperialist struggles (the Egyptian Wafd is a good example). Moreover, this democratic consciousness was confined within the narrow limits of bourgeois liberalism.

The dominant tendencies in the popular and radical movements of national liberation were marked more by their progressive social content than by the democratic tendencies of their militants, despite the sometimes ritualistic use of the term "democracy" and the advanced consciousness of segments of the avant garde. I do not believe that I am distorting reality when I say that the peasant-soldier who entered Beijing in 1949 was thinking of land reform, but was barely aware of the meaning of democracy. Today, his worker-son or daughter has wider aspirations. The same was true of the Egyptian peasant, even of the Wafd voter, and no doubt of many others.

But what kind of democracy are we talking about? This is hardly the place to disparage the heritage of Western bourgeois democracy: respect for rights and the rule of law, freedom of speech, institutionalization of electoral procedure, separation of powers, checks and balances, etc. But we should not stop there. Western democracy has no social dimension. People's democracies at moments of revolutionary social change—the USSR in the 1920s, Maoist China, etc.—have taught us a lot about what "people's power" should be, if we may allow this much-abused expression to take on its literal meaning. To stop at Western democratic forms without taking into consideration the social transformations required by the revolts of the periphery is to stop far short of what the people need. For democracy to take root, it must go beyond its merely capitalist form.

This is a prospect that imperialism finds impossible to accept. And this impossibility reveals the limits of the campaign of "democracy" the West has orchestrated—a campaign that equates democracy to multi-party politics. I would argue that Jacobin democracy was astonishingly modern. In each of the three great revolutions I have described, the play of ideas and social forces at moments of radicalization has succeeded in pushing far beyond the requirements of the "historically necessary" social transformation. Jacobin democracy, in short, did much more than merely establish the power of the bourgeoisie. It is the democracy to which the popular classes of the third world aspire, albeit in a confused manner. It is also clearly distinguishable from liberal bourgeois democracy, which ignores the dimensions of the necessary social reforms, just as it is distinguishable from the popular mobilizations to which we have referred, whose contempt for democracy stifled their potential for renewal.

My proposition certainly pays no heed to fashion. The latter seeks to devalue revolutionary radicalization in the name of realism, just as it looks to themes from another tradition, that of the "local democracy" familiar in English-speaking countries. Decentralization and the autonomy of a dismembered and segmented civil society are, in this spirit, proposed as realizable social advances. The trends in this direction are often tinged with religiosity, and seem to me to be too hostile to the state to constitute any real historical challenge.

There is something to be learned here, however, and a genuine dialogue is necessary. That being said, it is difficult to know nowadays whether the social movements at the periphery (and for that matter at the center) are capable of making headway in the face of the objective challenge. Some of these movements seem to be dead ends. This is true of the fundamentalist religious renewals and ethnic communal withdrawals. As symptoms of the crisis, not solutions, they will collapse as soon as they have revealed their impotence in the face of the real challenge.

Other movements, on the contrary, may have a real role to play in constructing a society that goes beyond capitalism and resolves the contradictions that really existing capitalism cannot. It seems to me that this will happen whenever the new movements (or the old ones) transcend the mere ambition to seize control of the state and instead announce an entirely different concept: the social power they intend to control. The question is not whether to struggle for power, but what kind of social power the struggle is being waged for. The organizations structured around the equation "power equals the state" will inevitably lose their legitimacy once the people take the measure of the state. Forms of organization stressing the complex social dimensions of power will become increasingly successful. In this connection the concept of nonparty politics may also prove fruitful.[9] The same may be said for anti-authoritarianism in Latin America; here, Pablo Casanova detects the defining characteristic of the new movements: rejection both of authoritarianism in the party and its leadership, and of dogmatism in ideology.[10] This is a reaction against the burdensome legacy of history; it will undoubtedly be conducive to progress. For the same reason, feminism in the West is in the vanguard of social liberation. Whether these advances imply going beyond capitalism or eventually can be absorbed by it remains to be seen. In the medium term they will challenge it but will not shake its foundations. Their longer–term future remains uncertain. It is not impossible that many of them will wither away in the current crisis.

Can objective criteria be defined to encourage history to move in the essential national and popular direction? I think so, and I make the following preliminary comments.

First: The principal task is to re-politicize the masses in a democratic direction. At one time they had a sense of independence to be regained. But once this aim was achieved, the language of national liberation movements lost its relevance and the movements themselves lost momentum. Can a repoliticization be extra-party or even anti-party? The question is open, although I personally am offended by what seems to be the paternalism underlying the activity of many of the trendy nongovernmental organizations.

Second: Democratic repoliticization of the people must be based on reinforcing their capacity for self-organization, self-development, and self-defense. Obviously the goal of self-development through various forms of cooperation, co-management, and popular management provokes conflict with the state, overt if the state is neocolonial, latent if it is embarked on a national and popular program which becomes the locus of objective class conflict. Might it be possible to transform activities now inaccurately described as "informal" into a "people's economy"? Under current conditions these activities are fully integrated into the global capitalist system and function either to reproduce the labor force at minimum cost or to supply inputs cheaply. They are necessary to the profitability of capitalism. Transforming them into a people's economy would be fraudulent if this conflict of interest were not faced openly.

Third: The kind of action envisioned here raises the question of relations between "the movement" and the parties of both the historical left and the populist struggle for independence. It seems to be neither proper nor correct to lump these parties—whatever their mistakes and historical limitations—with those responsible for neocolonial management. Similarly, the question arises anew of the relations between the movement and the new forces that have coalesced at one time or another on a national and progressive platform. I am thinking, obviously, of the organizations of anti-imperialist and progressive soldiers that responded to popular aspirations, even if the changes were inaugurated by *coups d'état* (Egypt, Jerry Rawlings' Ghana, Thomas Sankara's Burkina Faso, etc.).

Fourth: Analysis of the strategy of democratic repoliticization implies reopening at least three broad debates of theoretical significance:

—The role of the revolutionary intelligentsia as a social catalyst capable of drafting a concrete alternative plan and promoting the struggles for its implementation.

—The cultural content of this alternative plan—its potentially universalist scope, essential in my opinion, its relations with the national cultural heritage, etc.;

—The long-term outlook: socialism or capitalism?

Although it is fashionable nowadays to deny validity to such debates, I believe they are indispensable. Here I merely point them out, as I have discussed the details in other writings.

Fifth: Current history offers some tentative examples of movement in this direction. I am thinking, for example, of Sankara's Burkina Faso, but also of other movements even more abused by the dominant media of the West. Obviously the first steps fall short of solving the fundamental issues of the relationship between the authorities and the parties of the radical left, the relationship to populism, to the soldiers, etc. However, the debate on these issues must be opened.

Sixth: There are no magic formulas to substitute for democratic dialogue about goals among all the tendencies in the movement. I shall merely suggest that the major choice to be made is between the accumulation of national and individual wealth and the search for the welfare of the people. Marx's theory of the alienation intrinsic in the market economy, far from being played out, is being rejuvenated by its rediscovery by contemporary movements.

The current offensive of the Western powers and their media, ostensibly in support of democracy, has the merit of concealing its destabilizing tendencies. I deduce that it is not really a campaign for democracy, but an attack on socialism. The cause of democracy—as a means of stabilizing an alienated society—is being mobilized as a tactical weapon. And like all tactical weapons, it is being deployed with a grain of cynicism. What other explanation is there for the way the Western media, until recently so touchy about freedom of expression in the countries of really existing socialism, stand up for the Afghan Muslims who do not conceal their intention to close the schools (beginning with those for girls, of course) that the infamous secularists of Moscow dared to open? What other explanation is there for the way these media ignore the interventions of Western paratroopers coming to the aid of African dictators at the end of their tether?

The powers of the West are, in principle, neither for nor

against democracy, neither for nor against peace. They are driven by an all-determining fixation on maintaining an imperialist order that reserves to them the right to exploit all the riches of the planet for their own profit, to the detriment of its other peoples. If this order can be better served by a "democracy," they are for it, but they never hesitate to support or even install a dictator if this better serves their needs. If peace does not menace their imperial order, they are for peace. If it does, they choose a war as fierce as is necessary.

The people of the periphery, who are the victims of this never ending imperialism, have no choice but to struggle to bring it to an end by any means necessary. But there is something new going on. Victory in these struggles now requires a democratic conscience and practice more than ever before. The West was able to build itself without democracy of this sort (or, more precisely, before this sort of democracy had come on the political scene), and these nations for the most part were established by violence.

But once again history has demonstrated that it does not repeat itself. The first victories of national liberation created a new scenario in which the pursuit of these objectives required strong popular unity inconceivable without democracy. Yet the Western powers will not hear of democracy in these peripheral countries, so their propaganda machines busy themselves fighting against it. But if the democracy in question has become an essential element in the liberation of the third world, it is not a substitute for other elements, including economic and military power.

Moreover, it is the only factor absolutely essential for overcoming economic and military power. So, when all these conditions are fulfilled, then and only then will one be able to envision a new world order responsive to universal humanist values. Until that time, the world will be structured by an imperialist disorder founded on inequality among people.

Notes

1. Immanuel Wallerstein, in Samir Amin, Giovanni Arrighi, Andre Gunder Frank, and Immanuel Wallerstein, *Transforming the Revolution* (New York: Monthly Review Press, 1990).

2. Samir Amin, *Eurocentrism* (New York: Monthly Review Press, 1989).

3. Richard Sandbrook and Judith Barker, *The Politics of Africa's Economic Stagnation* (Cambridge: Cambridge University Press, 1985).

4. A. Erman and H. Ranke, *La civilisation égyptienne* (Paris, n.d.), pp. 201-202.

5. Samir Amin, *Class and Nation, Historically and in the Current Crisis* (New York: Monthly Review Press, 1980), Chap. 3.

6. Etiemble, *L'Europe chinoise* (Paris: Gallimard, 1985).

7. Samir Amin, *Class and Nation*, Chap. 2.

8. Ntalaja-Nzongola, *Revolution and Counter-Revolution in Africa* (London: Zed Books, 1988).

9. I refer here to the writings of the Indian economist Rajni Kothari.

10. Pablo Gonzalez Casanova, "El Estado y la política en America Latina," mimeographed (Dakar: Third World Forum, 1988).

5
THE REGIONAL CONFLICTS

In recent years the dominant media have repeated over and over that the East-West confrontation is winding down and that all local and regional conflicts can now find peaceable solutions in their turn. This position proceeds quite simply from the West's claim that the North-South conflict does not exist. To admit its existence would of course be to admit that the Western powers are imperialist and that their long-time aggression against the people of the periphery is in fact the principal cause of the conflicts in question. It would be to admit as well that the support the USSR sometimes lent to radical nationalism in the third world was not the real reason why the people of Asia, Africa, and Latin America questioned the imperialist order.

In opposition to the Western thesis I maintain that the conflict of the center and the periphery is primary, and that in consequence, the apparent victory of those who have sought to win over Moscow to the West will now occasion an intensification of the conflict in the third world.

This is what I predict: The West will attempt to establish its order by violence, without having to fear any further complications in its relations with the East. In their interventions, the Western powers will necessarily provoke an explosion of resistance on the part of the people of the third world but will no longer be able to claim that the troublemakers are agents of Moscow, as they did in the cases of Nasser in Egypt, the FLN in Algeria, the Viet Cong, the Sandinistas, and the followers of Nkrumah and Lumumba.

This scenario being the case, it appears necessary to open a new debate. That debate concerns violence and its characteristics as a social and political phenomenon, inasmuch as the current theorization surrounding it remains superficial and is in fact shot through with ideological distortions.

A Historical Materialist Theory of Conflicts

Social reality, considered as a whole, has three dimensions—economic, political, and cultural. The economy probably constitutes the best understood dimension, and bourgeois economics has forged tools to analyze it and (with more or less success) to manage capitalist society. Historical materialism has penetrated further and deeper; it has often been able to explain successfully the nature and extent of the struggles inherent in economic choice.

The areas of power and culture are considerably less well understood, and the eclecticism of the associated theories reflects the poor scientific mastery of reality.

Were one to write a theory of power, the first chapter might be titled, "The Fetishism of Power and the Secret Thereof." But no such work has been written; it remains a priority on the agenda of historical materialism.[1] Hence I begin with Lenin's dictum that "Politics is condensed economics." This proposition holds considerable truth, but it is important to delineate its limits. It only makes sense in the capitalist epoch. In precapitalist societies, the political and ideological instances predominate, and the formula should be reversed to say that "Economics is condensed politics." Lenin's formula, valid for capitalism, implies that the essence of capitalism is the fundamental class contradiction between bourgeoisie and proletariat, the social face of the contradiction between capital and labor that defines the capitalist mode of production. In that case, all politics, including the wars of the capitalist epoch, must ultimately derive from this fundamental conflict and the means used to resolve it.

But if we consider really existing capitalism as a world system, we place at center stage a further contradiction, the moving force behind real history—the opposition of the peoples of the periphery to the domination of international capital. Notice that I refer to "peoples," that is to say, a nonhomogeneous system of popular classes, and never nations, states, or even proletariats. Politics and wars are largely the products of this contradiction.

To take another step toward concrete analysis, one can seek to define how the "dominant capital" in question functions. Here I suggest that the key is to know how and at what point a national bourgeoisie, the constitution of its state, and the crystallization of its interests achieve correspondence; at least, this has been the key until the present day. The formation of nation-states in the center has corresponded to the emergence of numerous groups of bourgeoisie and national capitals. Under this scenario there are then several dominant capitals, and both politics and wars are determined largely by the conflicts among these capitals to decide who dominates the peripheral zones. In this sense, as Oliver Cox and (in a general sense) the world systems school have proposed, imperialism is a permanent trait of capitalism and not its highest stage, as Lenin believed.

But is this still true? The globalization thesis stresses those new tendencies which define the future in terms of an internationalization of capital beyond its national bases, thus generating for the first time in history a global capital and a global capitalism. From this standpoint, the correspondence between state and capital has disappeared, leaving in its stead a new contradiction between the multiplicity of states and the internationalization of capital. This being as it may, I nonetheless submit that the construction of a unified American-European-Japanese state is not likely in the foreseeable future. The contradiction will therefore remain and necessarily generate a new source of global disorder.

The West has historically viewed the socialist societies and states of the East as adversaries, which they were to the extent that the national popular construction they espoused would not submit to the needs of capital. Conscious of their weaknesses, these states aspired to "peaceful coexistence," to use their term. But the West saw in this weakness only an incentive to apply pressure in the hope of destroying the national popular vision. Depending on time and circumstance, these pressures reached the level of cold war, even outright war, although détente occasionally blunted their edge.

This long-lasting hostility toward the socialist societies and states has been paralleled in the West's attitude toward national liberation movements, which like socialism are disposed to lay really existing capitalism to rest. The third world states whose struggles for national liberation have become radicalized have actively resisted the West's efforts to reintegrate them into its sphere; the alliances of third world countries with the socialist bloc must be understood in this light. The era of such alliances has come to an end, at least for now. In the foreseeable future, the states of the third world will have to confront imperialism alone.

Conflicts in the Third World

Almost all regions of the third world are the sites of numerous and near-permanent conflicts. Their diversity and the apparent impossibility of finding solutions are so discouraging that many analysts give up trying, contenting themselves instead with analogies to a feudal Europe they do not understand either. In this view, third world societies are victims of their own backwardness and are the contested terrain of various tribes, groups, and communities. As such, they provide room for power contests among autocrats inclined to ally themselves with those great powers that want to further their own agendas.

The metaphor is facile; the vision, which gained ground when the illusions of the 1960s began to fade, remains false. Every case has its own peculiarities, which must not be ignored. In this sense, concrete analysis is irreplaceable. In almost every case, however, four sources of conflict combine in a unique pattern: **First**, the suppressed conflict between popular and national liberation and the logic of submission to imperialism. **Second**, the internal conflicts that arise from the fragility of national society, its popular forces, and its governing classes. **Third**, until recently, the East-West conflict, which expressed its own logic in the conflicts of the third world. **Fourth**, the commercial competition among those capitalists with interests in the regions in question.[2]

I present these sources of conflict in the order of their importance. This order reflects on the one hand the potential degree of violence attached to the source of the conflict, and on the other the consequent impact of a solution. Accordingly, the most violent wars in the third world, as a rule, are those where direct confrontation with imperialism occupies center stage. The wars of Central America and the Middle East are obvious examples.

According to this view, the South African struggle will not end simply with the abolition of apartheid, which has provided the basis for evolution in either of two contradictory directions. One, the strategic objective of the West, would stop with the realization of majority rule, implying a black government in South Africa disposed to play the game of integration into the world capitalist system. South Africa would then repeat the experience of Zimbabwe in the years after it achieved independence under the Lancaster House Agreement. The alternative prospect would involve an advance beyond neocolonialism. South Africa's material basis, unequalled on the continent, reinforces this possibility. Obviously, the prospect of this kind of progress threatens neocolonialism throughout southern Africa, to say the least.

As a result, Western strategy has a dual and not at all contradictory objective: on the one hand to use negotiations and pressure to eliminate apartheid before the struggle becomes so radical that it takes another direction; and on the other to accelerate the neocolonial reconquest of the fragile states in the surrounding region—Angola and Mozambique. The destabilization of these regimes, pursued in the past in collusion with apartheid South Africa, fits naturally into the West's strategy against national popular struggles. With the withdrawal of the Cubans, this destabilization has almost reached its objectives.

As in Palestine, the conflict in southern Africa illuminated the limits of Soviet involvement. It also revealed the united front that the West presents against national-popular liberation.

Obviously, the Middle East and South Africa do not exhaust the fields of conflict between national-popular aspirations and Western imperialism. Without exaggeration, one can say that the African continent as a whole constitutes the permanent and major theater of this conflict. In the course of the last three decades, at various times half the African states have reached beyond neocolonialism to independence. In varying degrees, all of their efforts have met with the hostility of the West, in forms ranging from economic and financial pressure to subversion and military intervention.

Doubtless, the national aspirations of the governments in question did not permit a uniform degree of radicalization. Often they lacked sufficient popular power, sometimes because the governments themselves did not want the popular movement to acquire dynamic autonomy. Moreover, these attempts sometimes seemed inherently weak, and they slid back into neocolonialism. Some could not surmount contradictions among their own people—ethnic conflicts, for example.

The economic and political apparatuses the Europeans established on the eve of independence were not designed to support popular governments, but to maintain the neocolonial order. There is little reason for surprise, therefore, that so many "rapid deployment" interventions were able to reinstall dictators committed to Western interests. Hypocrisy reigns whenever the West laments the present state of Africa and its people without acknowledging its own support for the most retrograde and corrupt politicians on the continent.

Central America is equally a theater of North-South conflict. Nicaragua's attempt at liberation, its advances and retreats,[3] along with the permanent war in Guatemala and the recently settled one in El Salvador, are sometimes hidden, sometimes open, like the repeated populist attempts in the Caribbean (Jamaica, Haiti, Grenada). Always, however, they are the visible signs of this hypocrisy. It goes without saying that despite the retreat of the Soviets, whose interventions had always been timid in the backyard of the United States, the struggles of the region will continue.

I add to this list the astonishing war in Afghanistan. Has the Soviet intervention there not been a model of its kind, an attempt to "export revolution" in the guise of annexing the country to Moscow's sphere of interest? In part, certainly. But only in part. How to explain that, contrary to the expectations of the West, the Kabul regime did not fall to the assaults of the Islamic fundamentalists (here allies of the West) on the day following the departure of Soviet troops? This fact demonstrates the existence of local democratic forces, just as it shows that the West, despite its hypocrisy, prefers fundamentalism in the Muslim world to anything else. It is "their thing," just as it is in Saudi Arabia and the Gulf.

I do not mean to imply that the wars in the third world, and particularly in Africa, have no dimension but anti-imperialism. The list of inter-ethnic conflicts, for instance, is as long as that of conflicts between African nationalism and the West. Many countries have been or remain theaters of violent internal conflict, even civil war. No less significant is the list of wars over boundaries and territorial ambitions, open or hidden. None of these has been fabricated by agents from outside the third world. The pronouncements of African governments to the effect that outsiders are to blame seem dubious, even when, as is often the case, various external forces cynically use the occasion to further their own strategic or tactical objectives.

Are such conflicts the inevitable consequence of some hostility inherent in all human communities? I think not, and propose an alternative interpretation.

The coincidence of state and nation during the formation of the capitalist centers produced a history unique to Western Europe. This peculiar history is reflected in the bourgeois ideological concept of the "nation." Its applicability even in Europe east of the Elbe and south of the Alps, and *a fortiori* in the rest of the world, is debatable. But the European ideology of ethnicity is in large part a by-product of its ideology of nation, and constitutes only a deformed and sometimes even fanciful view of reality.

In view of this, I propose the hypothesis that communal conflicts result fundamentally from conflicts among fractions of the world's ruling classes. The fragility of most of these classes is probably their most obvious characteristic, particularly in the periphery. Some are comprador classes constrained to operate within the narrow limits set by world capital. These may be merely bureaucracies—the apparatuses of a comprador state. But they may constitute a genuine comprador bourgeoisie, which at least has real economic interests of its own, however inferior its position in world capitalism. Other members of the ruling class may have nationalist aspirations, without managing to become the intelligentsia of an alliance of truly popular forces.

In any case, the different fractions of such classes face a strong temptation to enhance their power by mobilizing the people behind various symbols that are politically potent but do not threaten their own class rule. Both ethnic and religious symbols are well adapted for use in this kind of competition for power, and such symbols then become the conceptual world within which political arguments are carried out.

It is not some sort of ethnocentric atavism, therefore, that compels people to misapprehend the world outside their own lands and customs, to see it in terms of fanciful concepts; nor does some other form of atavism lead rulers to manipulate their people with threats of "foreign devils" that cause their troubles. The weakness of peripheral society as a whole, and particularly of its ruling classes, is responsible for the creation of such political discourse, and therefore responsible for the political action that results from its application.

The only solution for this unhappy situation lies in strengthening the societies in question, putting an end to their peripheralization, and providing the basis for a politics rooted in reality. The national-popular perspective here requires a strategy that is at once democratic and unitary. That is, it must work toward maintaining and even creating great territories and thus large states that are equal to the defiance that national-popular disengagement demands. At the same time, it must respect the diversity inherent in building these large territories. In this political perspective, the right of the people to rule themselves must be realized.

I shall not return here to the implications for the third world of conflicts among the superpowers, since it is an issue whose time has now passed. Nor shall I ruminate about the impact on the third world of competition among the three central poles of world capitalism, quite simply because this competition has not entailed political conflict in Africa, the Middle East, or elsewhere in the third world. Quite the contrary. The means that the United States, Europe, and Japan have at their disposal in this region have been used in compliance with one another. Europe and Japan are, as of now, perfectly in accord.

The Gulf War

The theses put forward in the present work had already been elaborated before August 1990, the outbreak of the conflict that was to become, six months later, the Gulf war. This struggle only confirmed their analysis while at the same time signalling the dimensions of the North-South conflicts to come.

Evidently the Western military intervention against Iraq had nothing to do with the defense of democracy or the rule of law. The nature of the Iraqi regime and the personality of Saddam Hussein were certainly not without importance, but they were secondary. Saddam Hussein had been supported by the West for twenty years, including ten years of criminal and fruitless combat with Iran, because he had continued to serve the interests of the West. Never had he been notably democratic. Was not the pretext of democracy a bit ridiculous anyhow, in a war to defend Saudi Arabia and restore the Emir of Kuwait? What about the massacre of the Kurds, one might ask. What about the massacre of these same Kurds in Turkey? When the parties to a massacre are part of the Western alliance, one must be careful not to speak of their crimes. The argument of "international law" was not much better. What did the West do to force Israel to respect (the recently revoked) UN Resolution 242, and to evacuate the territories it has illegally occupied for twenty years? When has the West challenged the illegal annexation of the Golan Heights and East Jerusalem? Was it not grotesque to see Turkey (allied with Greece) waxing indignant over the annexation of Kuwait while that same nation, Turkey, having lately ravaged Cyprus without a murmur from the West, declared the necessity for a war to establish democracy—in Iraq?

As I have said, the strategic objective of the Western powers in the Middle East has been, for half a century, to control the flow of oil, and that means the maintenance of disunity among the Arabs and the superarmament of Israel.

This is why the real objective of the war has always been to destroy the military and diplomatic potential of Iraq. We now almost have proof that the decision was taken by Washington and Tel Aviv around the month of May 1990. Had Israel been able to destroy Iraq by itself, this would have been allowed under some pretext or other, much as it was in the war against Egypt in 1967, planned by Washington and Tel Aviv in 1965. But because the Iran-Iraq war led the West to furnish Saddam Hussein with weapons that threatened the absolute military superiority of Israel, the destruction of Iraq had to be undertaken directly by the armed forces of the West.

The invasion of Kuwait, preceded by multiple provocations, only served as a pretext. We know now that this invasion was a trap set by Washington, into which Saddam—encouraged at least tacitly by the U.S. ambassador to Baghdad—fell headlong. By invading Kuwait, Saddam upset the equilibrium that guaranteed the survival of the Gulf regimes. These countries, never admired by Arab opinion, were tolerated, thanks to the money they distributed and the massive immigration they absorbed. They were able, at least at the level of rhetoric, to proclaim an Arab nationalist position while, with the West's support, financing Islamic fundamentalist currents, thereby undermining the cause of the Arabs and Palestinians.

On August 2, 1990, therefore, no diplomat worthy of the title was really surprised, even if some pretended to be. At no moment in the phase of diplomatic initiatives did the Western powers propose credible terms for a collective discussion of the structure of the world order, which would have to include the right of Palestine to exist as a state and the right of the Arab people to use their oil wealth for their own benefit. Up until August 12, Saddam Hussein urged negotiations on a constellation of problems: Kuwait, Palestine, and the uses of the oil wealth in the region. The Western diplomats presented a united front of unqualified refusal because they had already decided on war.

The war in the Gulf was therefore truly a "North-South" conflict. From the point of view of the fundamental conflict of really existing capitalism, the 1980s had been a drab period of retreat of popular forces on a world scale. They had been marked, first of all, by a crumbling, then a collapse, of the tentative radical nationalisms of the Nasser type, which had their period of ascension during the 1950s and 1960s. On the same plane, the left in the West in these years rallied in varying degrees to the politics of neoliberalism—Reaganism, Thatcherism, and the like. And last, but by no means least, there was the collapse of the Communist regimes of Eastern Europe and the Soviet Union.

Under such circumstances, we were subjected in the last half of the 1980s to an enormous offensive of international capital whose aim was to subjugate the political and economic systems of the third world to the simple logic of the expansion of capital. This offensive was preceded by the Contra war in Nicaragua. There was the invasion of Grenada, to install a regime in the pay of the United States. And there was the invasion of Panama, which was certainly complicated by the character of the president of that country, but nonetheless had as its goal the maintenance of U.S. domination over a region it regards as "strategic." There were also numerous interventions in Africa, notably French, aimed at keeping in power men not known for their democratic tendencies. We were therefore in a period of reflux, where it seemed that the compradorization of the third world, accepted by its ruling classes, would function effectively.

Then, suddenly things exploded, admittedly under complex circumstances, but the essence of the matter was control over the oil of the Arab world.

The Present Situation

As I write, one can perceive the international order being imposed on the region, or in any case the order that the Western powers are trying to establish.

First, it is evident that they would like to keep control of the oil. But what price will they pay to guarantee this? In my judgment their military presence in the region will prove to be indispensable, for the petroleum nations of the Gulf now know that they cannot continue as independent states except under the direct and permanent protection of the Western armies. But this signifies that the complete collapse of the whole archaic system is inevitable, because in one manner or another the military occupation of the region is destined to end one day. In the meantime, will it be possible for the Western powers to substitute for direct military occupation a system of collective security arrangements that mask their presence behind regional treaties? The United States always tries to set up systems of this sort.

That is why we are seeing the reappearance of the old United States-European regional military pact among the comprador regimes of the area (called CENTO, for Central Organization, during the 1950s and 1960s). This arrangement invites the West to guarantee the status quo, prolonging NATO in this manner by giving apparent legitimacy to its interventions. We remember that CENTO was presented as anti-Soviet, while its role in protecting the imperialist status quo was partially masked by anticommunist rhetoric. Nevertheless, although the Soviet Union is no longer an enemy, the CENTO project has again popped to the surface. In the same manner elsewhere, the Alliance for Progress in Latin America, the EC-ACP for Sub-Saharan Africa, and the ASEAN for Southeast Asia were established as a network of domination by the West, complementary to its own organizations (such as NATO) and not in conflict with them. A new world order? Or an attempt to prolong the life of the old and to exploit the weakness of the USSR?

The Palestinian conflict complicates the other problems of the region and makes the likelihood of a peaceable solution less probable than ever. I shall not expand on the deep nature of this conflict, but instead refer the reader to other writings on the subject.[4] It is vital to understand that the Palestinian conflict is not just the collision of two nationalisms—Arab and Israeli—whose legitimacies are equivalent. For Israel is an instrument in the service of the global expansion of capital, whose objective is to put a stop to all national and popular revolutions of the Arab people. Foreign aggression against such Arab renewal, on whose behalf Israel has been the favored instrument for forty years, has effectively succeeded until now. But such a strategy of aggression is nothing new. Europe has set itself in a particularly relentless way against any attempt to modernize Egypt. And there are specific reasons why, no doubt attached to geopolitical strategy (yesterday the region's position on the route to India, today its proximity to oil), and to history (the deep fear on the part of the Europeans lest there arise on their southern flank a unified and modern Arab state under the influence of Egypt, uniquely capable of making this happen).

I have pointed out that it was not by mere chance that as long ago as 1839 (when the armies of Mohamed Ali defeated the Ottoman Sultan), British diplomacy invented the Israeli project. The object was to create a "European" state by organizing Jewish immigration to Palestine, to keep an eye on Egypt, and to bisect the Arab East—as the London *Globe* wrote at the time. The *Globe* piece was published fully forty years before the first manifestations of Zionism. Yet today it still remains true that any mention of this aspect of Zionism is drowned out by the same chants of anti-Semitism that greet any criticism of Israel.

At the same time, the Palestinian conflict revealed the limits of the alliance between the Arab national liberation movement and the Soviet Union. The latter was always careful to subordinate its support for anti-imperialist struggles to its global and permanent strategy of peaceful coexistence. But in any case, the USSR has had a change of policy and no longer plays a role in the region, at least for now. Can one then deduce that conditions are ripe for peace? I think not, first of all because when confronting the Palestinian conflict, the differences within the West lose their sharpness. Despite the economic competition between the United States and Europe, the entire West has lined up behind the United States on this issue. No doubt at certain times General de Gaulle hoped to endow Europe, that is, France, with a margin of autonomy, partially reflected in an Arab politics free from subjugation to the dictates of Zionism. But such inclinations were never really pursued.

At the present time Zionism can expect to follow its trajectory of maximal expansion without hindrance. Despite the ceaseless intonations of the media on the menace to Israel, for fifty years the principal victims of power politics in the region have been the Palestinian people, not Israel. Sustained by the United States and Europe, unconditionally and massively, financially and militarily, Israel has been able as a consequence to recapitulate in the twentieth century the history of colonial conquest in the nineteenth, driving an entire people from its homeland. With all the arrogance that this Western support permits, Israel has launched daily aggressions against the Arab people, and bombarded Libya, Tunisia, and Iraq with impunity. Its army has sunk to crushing the hands of Palestinian children who write on the walls. But it is not difficult to find excuses. Israel is otherwise a "democratic" country, is it not? Was Shamir not elected? And so on. Any time the victims of Zionism protest their extermination, there is a rush to support the continuing expansion of their exterminators.

Is it a product of the Arab imagination that the dominant opinion in the United States and Europe evades the issue in such a shameful way? I wish to say on this matter that the shame of anti-Semitism which culminated in Hitler's genocide has found its match in the West's cynical use of the descendants of Hitler's victims to carry out its imperialist designs in the Near East.

But imagine that at the end of the Gulf war the United States had been able to impose "peace" in the region. In perfect consonance with the Zionist project, the area would have been broken up into a scattering of states, in a generalized "Lebanonization." Suppose too that the U.S. Army had taken direct control of the petroleum fields and that the governments of the region, totally disarmed, had been left without power, that the people—demoralized for a time— had accepted generalized compradorization and themselves offered to Israel the role of intermediary between imperialist capital and the local bourgeoisie. Even then, can one imagine for a moment that the people of the region, Arabs and Iranians, would have indefinitely accepted this new order?

The conflict in the Gulf has given tragic evidence of the limits of the hope placed on an alternative European perspective on the world order, detached from that of the Atlantic alliance. For this reason, the European project is weakened, and the blow that the United States has delivered by taking the initiative in the Gulf has weakened it further. For it is now clear that the United States will use its military control over the oil of the Gulf to impose its politics, even on Europe. It is necessary therefore to develop in counterpoint a new long-term political strategy that takes account of the new givens in Germany and Eastern Europe—to aim at constructing de Gaulle and Gorbachev's vision of one Europe. And it is necessary to reinforce this perspective by supporting progressive and democratic forces that can advance a solution to the problems of the Arab world in particular and the South in general.

Does the responsibility for the European checkmate fall upon the pro-Western turn of Gorbachev's successors? This cannot be certain. If the Europeans, that is to say the French, had adopted a stronger position, daring to confront the United States, it is probable that the Soviets and Chinese would have followed. For if Gorbachev was not in a position to confront simultaneously the United States and Europe, he could have taken a different position if he had felt he was being supported by Europe. If France had not withdrawn its proposition from the Security Council on January 14, 1991, there would have been a veto, but the United States and Britain would have found themselves isolated. In fact, French diplomacy rendered a fine service to the Americans.

Things being as they are, will this post-Gulf war era inaugurate, for a time, a return to the hegemony of the United States that we too hastily declared to be over? I do not think so. In fact the war ended in the consolidation of a triumvirate of the United States, Japan, and Germany (meaning Germany, not Europe). Japan and Germany, which largely financed the war, will pay the U.S. gendarme charged with maintaining the order necessary to unify the world by means of the market. On the side of this triumvirate, I see weak countries like the USSR, marginalized countries like France, and compradorized countries like the majority of the third world. I call this order which is taking shape for the intermediate period to come, the "empire of chaos."

It is not in fact a question of the construction of a new world order and is in fact a little better than the one which emerged in the aftermath of the World War. It is nevertheless a sort of military framework to accompany the savage order of neoliberal capitalism; a theory of low intensity conflicts has already been produced by American experts to this effect.

And while I do not know if the war in the Gulf shows that the North-South conflicts inherent in this conception have already passed the "threshold" of intensity under consideration, I strongly believe that the years to come will show only that really existing capitalism is barbarism.

And in its new neoliberal garb that means nothing more than barbarism without limits.

Notes

1. Samir Amin, *Eurocentrism* (New York: Monthly Review Press, 1989), pp. 1-11.

2. Samir Amin, *Maldevelopment: Anatomy of a Global Failure* (London: Zed Press, 1990), Chap. 4, Sec. 3. Cf. in particular my remarks on the South African and Palestinian conflicts and the Soviet interventions in Africa. See also pp. 90-95 on the question of ethnicity.

3. Xavier Gorostiaga, *La Transición Difícil* (Managua, 1987).

4. Cf. Amin, *Maldevelopment*. Also Amin, *Eurocentrisme et politique*, IFDA, dossier N° 65. (Genève, 1988); and Faysal Yachir, *The Mediterranean: Between Autonomy and Dependency* (London: Zed Books, 1989).